Powers That Be

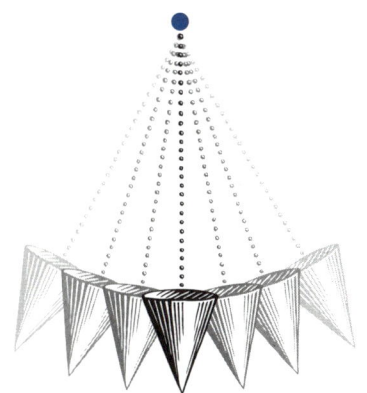

Powers That Be

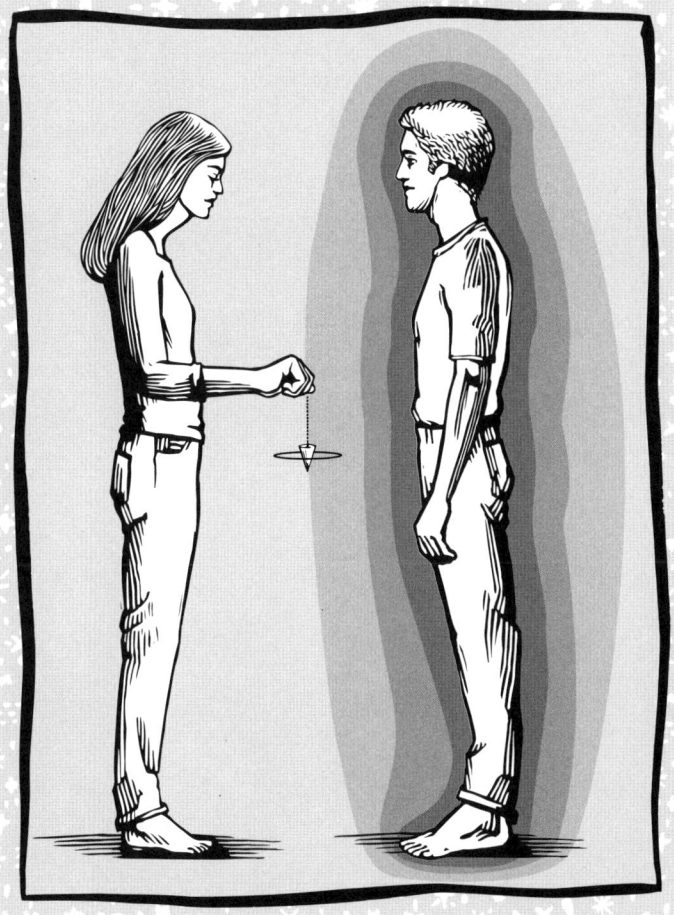

By Walter Woods
with Marin Gazzaniga

BEAUX ARTS EDITION

Copyright © 2000 Hugh Lauter Levin Associates, Inc.
Beaux Arts Edition

ISBN: 0-88363-910-6

Design: Kathleen Herlihy-Paoli, Inkstone Design
Illustrations: Joanna Yardley

Thank you to Marin Gazzaniga for her skill with words and language,
to Joanna Yardley for her excellent illustrations,
to Kathleen Herlihy-Paoli for the attractive design,
to Deborah Zindell for her fine copy editing,
to Leslie Carola for her superb guidance, editing, and publishing abilities.

Printed in China

I'd like to dedicate this work to the hundreds
of kindred souls who over the years
have shared their personal experiences,
observations, and insights,
and to everyone who worked on this project.

CONTENTS

Introduction......8

SEEING AURAS...11
WHAT IS AN AURA?......13
STRONG AND WEAK AURAS......17
AURAS OF MANY COLORS......19
SEEING YOUR FIRST AURA......21
TRAINING YOUR EYES TO SEE AURAS......21
SEEING A PERSON'S AURA......23
STRENGTHENING YOUR AURA......26
Kirlian photography......28

DOWSING...31
WHAT IS DOWSING?......33
HOW DOES DOWSING WORK?......34
WHO CAN DOWSE?......37
GETTING STARTED......38
THE INSTRUMENTS......38
L-rods......39
The pendulum......40
The bobber......41
The Y-rod......42
PROGRAMMING YOUR DOWSING SYSTEM......44
THE QUESTION......45

DOWSING WITH L-RODS...49
ASKING FOR PERMISSION OR GUIDANCE......53
Yes/no practice questions......54
FINDING A LOST OBJECT......55
FINDING THE FLOW OF WATER......58
DOWSING THE AURA......60
Ley lines and earth powers......62
FENG SHUI......63

PENDULUM DOWSING...65
PROGRAMMING YOUR PENDULUM......67
DOWSING FOR INFORMATION......70

Dowsing for noxious zones......71
READING MAPS WITH A PENDULUM......73
A FINAL WORD: BE WARY......75

CHAKRAS...77

CHAKRAS AND THE AURA......79
THE SEVEN CHAKRAS......81
Root or base chakra......81
Sacral or navel chakra......81
Solar plexus chakra......81
Heart chakra......84
Throat chakra......84
Brow or third eye chakra......85
Crown chakra......85
Colors of the chakras......82
TESTING THE CHAKRAS......86
BALANCING THE CHAKRAS......87

LABYRINTHS...89

WHAT IS A LABYRINTH?......91
DRAWING A SEED PATTERN......92
DRAWING THE CLASSICAL 7-CIRCUIT LABYRINTH......94
COLORING THE LABYRINTH......97
HOW TO MAKE A LABYRINTH......98
WALKING THE LABYRINTH......98
USING THE LABYRINTH TO SOLVE PROBLEMS......99

MIND AND BODY POWERS...103

THE ENERGY IN YOUR HANDS......105
HEALING A HEADACHE WITH YOUR HANDS......106
LEVITATING WITH YOUR FINGERTIPS......107
MIND OVER MATTER......111
The truth within your arms......112
DEVELOPING ESP......115
Edgar Cayce......116

Conclusion......119

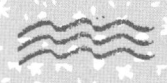

INTRODUCTION

All of us have heard or told stories about incredible occurrences that seem to defy logical explanation—women who are easily able to lift a car to save a child who is trapped underneath, "water witches" who can discover underground sources of water simply by following the pull of Y-shaped tree branches, people who can walk across burning hot coals without feeling any pain or showing any evidence of burns or blisters. These amazing feats seem to be beyond our human understanding. But are they?

Extraordinary human powers, the phenomenon of dowsing, the auras of the body's energy centers, these ideas are not the types of concepts that, in our culture, intelligent people are supposed to find credible. By simply following the activities in this book, however, you will begin to experience some of these phenomena firsthand and will start to understand the principles on which many unusual practices and beliefs are based.

Powers That Be and the companion components will teach you how to see colored auras and measure them with an L-rod tool. You will learn to gauge the strength of chakras (the body's energy fields) with a pendulum, and even to perform feats of incredible strength, using just your fingertips. As you become more aware of the powers in the world around you—and the powers within you—you will start to think twice about the amazing stories and phenomena that you may once have considered impossible and strange.

Is it really so hard to believe that there might be mysterious powers and invisible energies in the world around us? Just think about it. There are so many simple, everyday examples that are already quite familiar to us. For example, a dog can hear certain high-pitched sounds that humans cannot. Radio waves are in the air all the time, but unless you have a radio, you cannot hear them. Humans simply don't have the necessary tools to perceive all of these sounds and frequencies—although some people have been able to pick up radio stations on their tooth fillings! With the right tools—or by attuning the tools that we

INTRODUCTION

already have—we, too, can detect many unseen wonders in the world around us that we otherwise could not observe.

Even with all of our modern-day scientific knowledge and advanced technology, many simple phenomena—such as dowsing and various types of extrasensory perception—may still be unexplained, although much progress has been made. In fact, we cannot be sure that all of what we now accept as scientific truth is even correct. Sherwin Nuland, author and winner of the National Book Award, is a distinguished surgeon and professor of medicine at Yale University in New Haven, Connecticut. He still recalls that during his first day as a medical student, his professor told the class: "Within ten years, 50 percent of what you will be learning now in medical school will be outdated, and 40 percent will be wrong." Science is an ongoing process of discovery—and there is still much that we have to learn.

The concepts of auras, chakras, and dowsing date back thousands of years. Of course, just because these ideas are old, does not necessarily mean they are accurate. It does mean, however, that these concepts have had a deep significance to generations of people and cultures who have passed them down through the centuries to us today. Whether or not they are scientifically explained, we should look closely at them for the kernels of truth that may lie within each one.

The *Powers That Be* set will give you a brief introduction to the concepts of auras, chakras, and dowsing, along with some interesting research, and the simple tools you need to begin exploring these phenomena. Approach the book and activities with an open mind and the spirit of fun. You will be astounded by what you will discover. Once you have experienced first hand the "powers that be," you will forevermore see the world in a slightly different way.

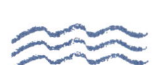

CHAPTER ONE

SEEING AURAS

"The idea of visible energy fields that extend beyond a person's body is not really new or far-fetched."

SEEING AURAS

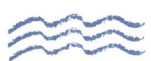

We have certainly all heard about people who are able to see auras, the energy fields of various colors that surround people, animals, and even objects. The word *aura* is from the Greek word *aer* (the source of the English word *air*), meaning "a subtle, sensory stimulus" and "the distinctive atmosphere surrounding a source."

For hundreds of years, religious art and icons have depicted the most holy figures—Moses, Vishnu, Buddha, Mary, Jesus, Mohammed, other prophets, and angels—as having halos around their heads and bodies. Sometimes, these circles of light are silver or gold; sometimes, they are made up of the many colors of the rainbow. Why did all these various artists depict auras? There surely must have been a reason why the same idea occurred to hundreds of artists in different cultures. Perhaps the idea of visible energy fields that extend beyond a person's body is not really that new or far-fetched.

WHAT IS AN AURA?

Life is energy. Centuries ago we had no way of knowing that things like radio waves, brain waves, light waves, and electricity existed. Today we can measure those forces and prove they exist with machines. But just because we couldn't "see" them before doesn't mean they didn't exist. Is it so hard to believe that there are other energy forms—things we can tune in to with our minds, or bodies—that we don't yet understand or know how to measure?

Science has proven that there are many types of invisible energy fields in the world around us. Newton's law of universal gravitation, for example, explains that there is a force of gravity between all objects relative to the size of the objects and their distance from one another. The intensity of the gravitational energy of a person or object does not compare with that of the earth, but any physicist would agree that gravitational energy extends beyond the physical form of every person and object.

Heat energy also radiates from living objects. The invisible energy we feel when we are close to a warm person is evidence enough of this phenomenon, but external body temperature does of course vary. The human body, which has an internal temperature of 98.6 degrees F is comfortable in air that is 70 degrees F, but the body feels much colder in water of that same temperature. Why? Is this phenomenon related to the fact that heat is absorbed more easily by water than air? It follows, therefore, that radiating body heat is insulated more effectively by cold air than by cold water.

Our bodies can also sense things at a great distance away by our awareness of the presence of other invisible influences. Even though humans do not have the highly developed olfactory sense of dogs, we can detect scents without directly smelling the object giving off the scent, whether the odor is as pleasant as a nearby field of flowers or as distinctive as a skunk at a distance.

That there are invisible gravitational, heat, and scent fields that extend beyond each person is commonly accepted. The human body is an energy system made up of all these different types of energy: heat, electrical, electro-magnetic, and sound are just a few. Is it then so difficult to believe that there may be other types of invisible fields that we may not as casually perceive?

Many believe that we can train ourselves to see some of these energy fields emanating from the body, and that what we may see is the aura that artists have been depicting for centuries. In fact, some sophisticated photographic processes have been able to detect what are normally invisible energy fields around the bodies of plants, vegetables, trees, animals, and humans. Isn't

Facing page: Although there are several layers to an aura, many dowsers are most successful concentrating on seeing the etheric layer and the astral layer (which consists of several layers itself).

Seeing Auras

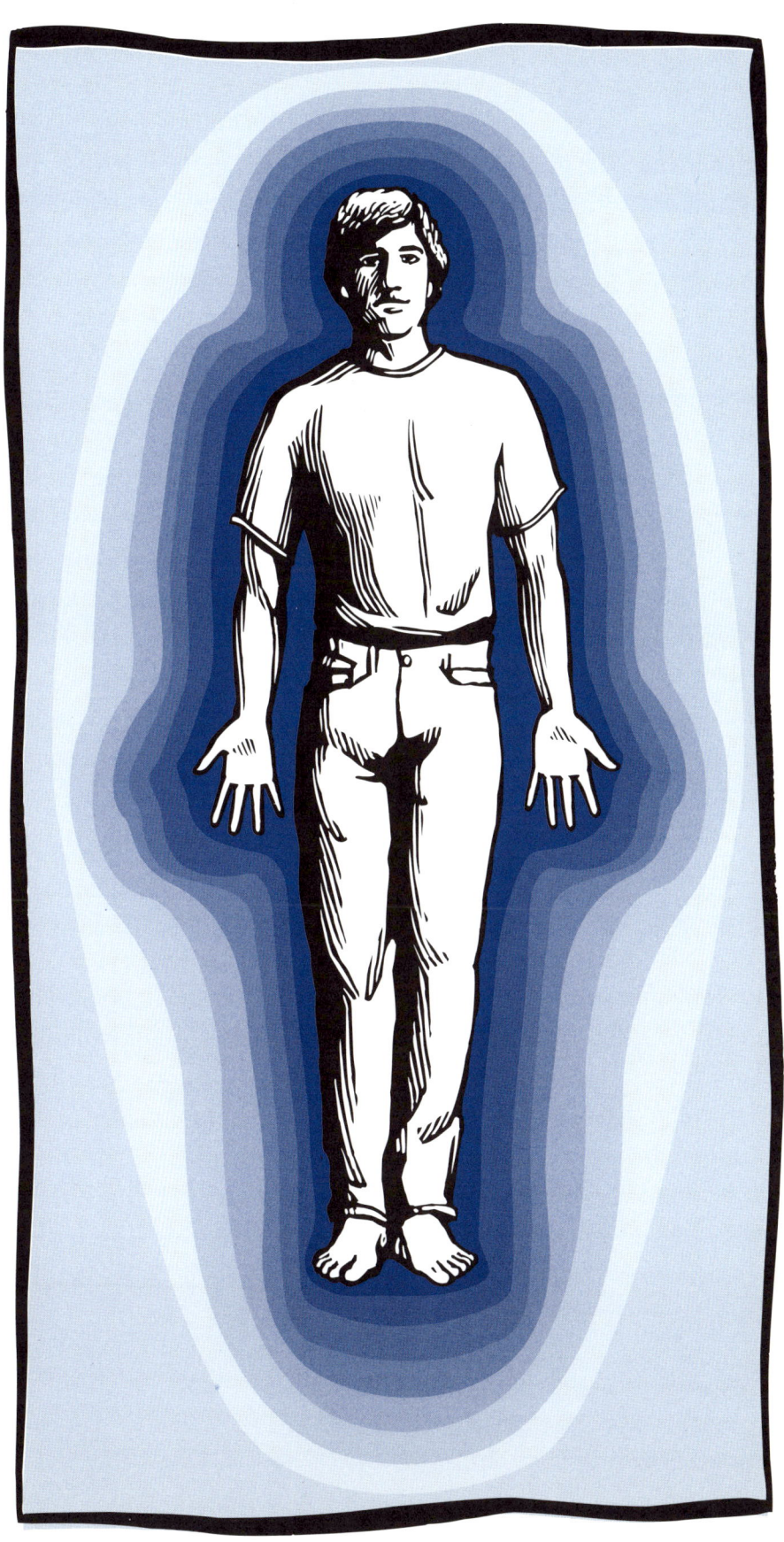

it possible that we can train ourselves to observe these same energy fields (auras) with the naked eye?

There are several auric layers. Most people can train themselves to see about three. When you are first learning, the aura you see will likely be the first one—the body aura. It can take a while to see each aura distinctly. Each auric layer represents a different aspect of human life. For instance, the first layer, the etheric or body aura, represents the physical; it reflects a body's physical health or weakness. It is usually close to the body, a thin band around one-eighth to one-quarter of an inch, although it can sometimes appear much larger. When you first learn to see an aura, this layer is usually visible as a somewhat clear but quite dense band, with an easily seen outer edge that may appear as a line between a person's body and what looks like the beginning of the next aura. Next to the etheric aura is the astral aura, which is believed to reflect the emotional and mental states of a person. (This aura is actually made up of several layers, but most people cannot differentiate each layer.) As you can imagine, an aura that reflects emotional and mental states can change from minute to minute! This layer extends from the body aura to anywhere from four inches to ten or more inches. When you first see the astral aura, it tends to look silvery or translucent. Eventually, as your skills develop, you will begin to see colors. The third layer is said to reflect a person's spirituality, and is the hardest to see.

All auras emanate from and surround the entire body. The reason you can see them separately is because of their different densities and the fact that they are superimposed on each other. The inner edge of the less dense, larger astral aura is visible at the point where the more dense first body aura stops, and the inner edge of the least dense third aura is seen where the astral aura stops. More auras extend farther from the body, but most people cannot learn to see much beyond these three. This book will teach you to dowse all three of these auras.

Facing page: A strong aura—all three layers—extends elliptically around the body. Note that the layers smooth out as they are farther from the body. The first layer is closest to the body and hugs its contours, while the outer layers offer a looser shape.

STRONG AND WEAK AURAS

If an aura is the reflection of the different energies we project, it follows that there must be strong and weak auras. No doubt you've heard someone say, "I really like her energy," or, "I got a bad vibe from that guy." Likely, you've had the experience of meeting someone and getting an immediate sense of them—some people attract attention the minute they walk into a room, others go unnoticed, still others can make people start to feel tired or uncomfortable—people can quite literally bring a room's energy up, or sap it dry. What are we talking about when we say such things? We can sense when someone has a strong or weak

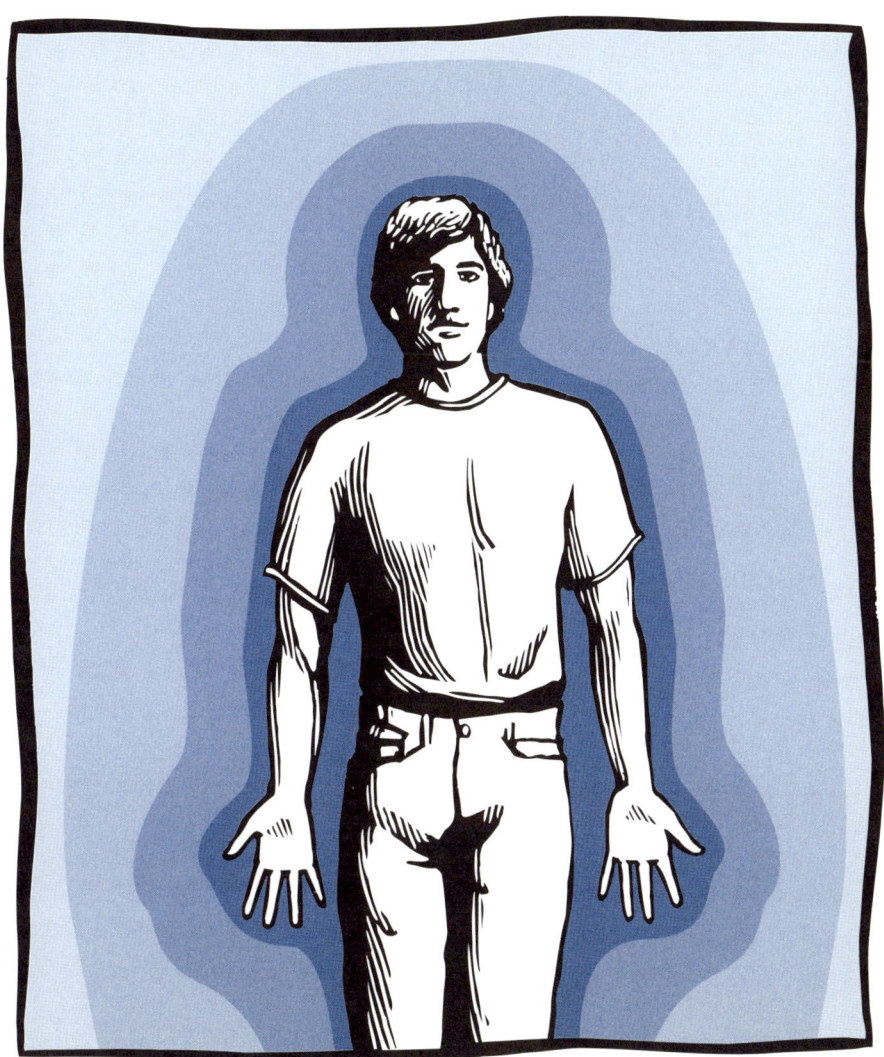

A weak aura—all visible layers—can appear uneven, hard-edged, or small. Just as a strong aura usually denotes good health, the weak aura can indicate imbalances or weakened resistance as a result of unhealthy diet, or poor sleep or exercise habits. Weak auras can be strengthened by correcting poor habits.

aura, because we can actually sense or feel the energy.

A strong aura is a healthy aura, meaning it reflects strong physical, mental, emotional, and spiritual energies. A healthy human aura is elliptical: a three-dimensional egg-shape surrounding us. Generally, the first three layers of healthy auras tend to extend from four to ten feet beyond the body, but they can reach much farther, as will be demonstrated later in this chapter. The halo, the part of the aura around the head, is said to be the most easily seen part of an aura, and can indicate a strong spiritual energy. In general, the stronger, healthier, and more vibrant a person's energy, the bigger their aura.

You can also see a weak or unhealthy aura: it can appear to be dented or uneven, no longer as rounded and full. It is also often much smaller than the strong aura, and the colors can be drab. Weak auras can indicate imbalances or problems with certain areas. Generally, weak auras are the result of a body energy that is out of whack due to poor habits or health. For instance, a bad diet, not getting enough proper exercise, fresh air, or sleep, the excess use of alcohol, tobacco, or drugs, or high levels of stress can all weaken a person's aura. Of course, this goes both ways: an aura can be strengthened relatively easily by improving habits in these areas (see page 26).

A weak aura not only reflects dis-ease, it can actually make a person more tired—energy is more easily drained when someone's aura is weak. Without the defense of a strong aura, a person's resistance is weakened. He or she is more vulnerable to disease, to fatigue, even to being treated badly by others. It is as if the aura is a protective shield and once it is weakened, harmful forces can attack us.

AURAS OF MANY COLORS

It can take a while for many people to see the colors in auras; others see colors right away. While you may have heard people say that someone's aura is red, or blue, or yellow, the colors of a person's aura actually change constantly, depending on their thoughts and feelings at a particular moment, their environment, or their health. However, we do tend to have a base color, particularly for the astral aura. This base color represents our dominant personality traits and is like the background color of a painting upon which our moods and thoughts are added in a range of colors.

People continue to argue about what exactly a particular color means, but there are generally accepted interpretations. If you think about it, we already have certain ideas about colors, ideas that seem to be so universal that they've become part of our everyday language—"He was green with envy"; "I was so mad, I was seeing red"; "Stay away from him today, he's in a black mood." Here are some basic guidelines: For example, a pretty rosy, clear red is positive; a dark, angry red is negative.

- **RED:** (as positive) passion, power, leadership; (as negative) nervous, aggressive, self-centered
- **ORANGE:** (as positive) harmonious, creative, intuitive; (as negative) worrisome, vain, lazy
- **YELLOW:** (as positive) intellectual, enthusiastic; (as negative) timid, overly critical, untruthful
- **GREEN:** (as positive) trustworthy, compassionate, peace-loving; (as negative) rigid, jealous, mistrustful.
- **BLUE:** (as positive) calm, devoted, sincere; (as negative) blocked, oversensitive, forgetful, impatient
- **VIOLET (indigo):** (as positive) intuitive, healing, nurturing, spiritual; (as negative) overbearing, self-important.

Of course there are other colors, but this gives you a start. In general, the colors you see that are closest to the body tend to reflect physical traits, and the colors that are farther out reflect mental, emotional, or spiritual traits. Clear, bright colors reflect high energy in those areas. Murky colors can indicate weakness, illness, or a problem area. Like everything in life, too much of a good color or trait (colors appearing muddied or overpowering) can turn positive qualities into negative qualities. It all depends on maintaining a good balance.

If you can develop your vision to the point where you can begin to see colored auras, think about the significance of the color that each person is emanating. But be careful you don't read too much into the colors you see in someone's aura, especially when you are just starting out. For one thing, what you see one day, may change the next—or even within minutes. And it takes years to develop the ability to discern the many subtleties involved in order to give a true auric reading. For now, have fun seeing whatever colors you can, and asking yourself whether those colors match up with what you know about the person!

SEEING YOUR FIRST AURA

The first auras you see will probably look more like a nearly clear or grayish haze. Remember: be patient. It takes consistent practice to discern colors. The following exercises will help train your eyes to be able to see auras. And keep in mind, the most important thing for learning to see an aura, is believing that you can see one!

TRAINING YOUR EYES TO SEE AURAS

Learning to soft focus your eyes is crucial for learning to see auras. Here are some exercises to help train (or maybe I should say "untrain") your vision. Place an 8 x 10-inch sheet of white paper on the surface of a table. Place the hot pink 3-inch square of paper from your kit in the center of the sheet.

Put your hand as close to your eyes as you can while still being able to focus on it clearly (usually about six inches away from your face). Now, maintaining the same focus that you have while looking at your hand closely, look at the pink square of paper, which should be about three feet away from you. Because you are maintaining a close focus, but looking at a more distant object, everything within your vision should be blurred except your hand. The farther-away items are in "soft focus." If what you see is not blurred, unfocus your eyes until it is.

Continue looking at the pink square with unfocused eyes for a full forty-five seconds (set an egg timer—placed far enough away so it doesn't interfere with your concentration—have a friend time you, or simply count to forty-five yourself). What do you see? Do you see a bright green color extending from the edges of the pink square? If not, start over again, this time looking at the paper for sixty seconds. It's hard to keep your eyes unfocused for this length of time, but if you can, you will most likely see the color green emanate around the edges of the paper. Even people with some forms of color blindness can see it.

Now, soft focus your eyes again and look at the pink square for forty-five to sixty seconds. When the time is up, slowly remove the pink paper, continuing to look at the area where the pink paper was and keeping your eyes unfocused. Now what do you see? Where did that green square come from? Green is the complementary color of pink. The green square that you see on the white paper is the *afterimage* of the pink square that was there.

Try this activity again, using the different colors of paper squares in the kit. You will always see each square's complementary color around it and in its place on the sheet of white paper when you remove it. A blue square will have an orange afterimage; a purple square will have a yellow afterimage. If you wear glasses, try this activity both with and without wearing your lenses to see which technique works best for you.

This method of training your eyes to soft focus will help you as you begin to train yourself to see auras around people.

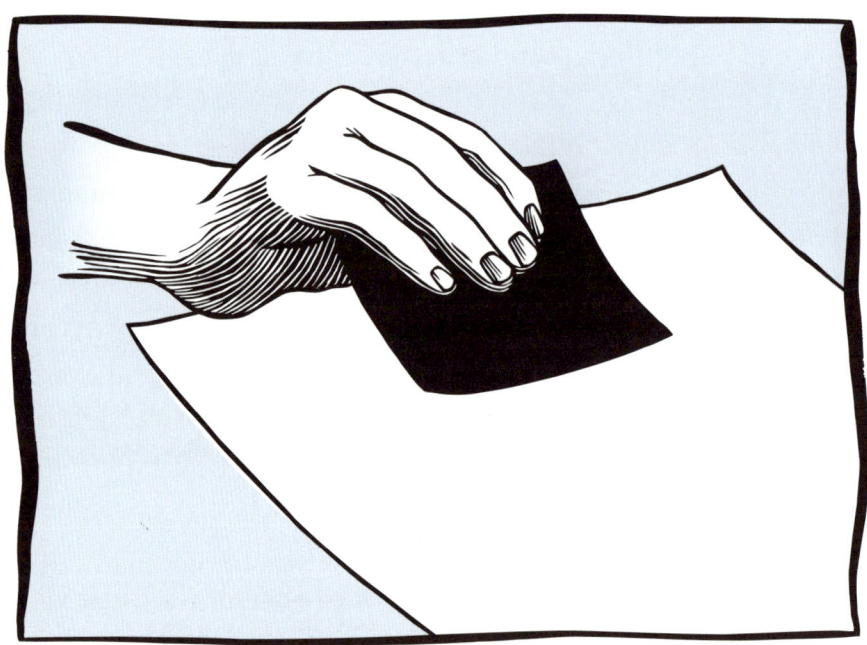

After staring at the hot pink square for about a minute, remove it from the surface of the white paper and you will see its "aura," which will be a "glow" of bright green where the pink paper had been. Greens are the complementary colors to red tones in the spectrum.

SEEING A PERSON'S AURA

You will need an assistant for this second experiment. (You are still training your eyes to prepare you to see auras; you are not actually seeing them . . . yet!) Tape a large bright colored sheet of paper (any bright one will do) on an evenly and indirectly lit, shadowless white wall. Natural light coming from the side is the best kind of light to use for this experiment; avoid overhead fluo- rescent light. Now, stand back from the wall at least ten feet or more and stare at the paper with soft-focused eyes for forty-five to sixty seconds. Keeping your unfocused gaze on the paper, ask your assistant to slowly remove the paper. Now, ask the person to stand in front of the area of the wall where the paper was taped. Keep your eyes softly focused on that area. What has happened to the red aura? Does it extend beyond the body of the person? What shape is it? Does the person's body affect the size and shape of the colored image?

Now try the same experiment with different colors of paper and different people. Do the density of color and the size and shape of its images change for different people and different colors? After you have tried these experiments, you are now ready to try to see auras without using colored squares!

Ask your assistant to stand one to two feet away from the white wall. You stand at least ten feet away from your partner and, with unfocused eyes, stare at the wall beyond his or her head and shoulders. Do you see a fuzzy, silvery, or translucent band that is about two inches wide, give or take, all around the person? This is your first aura! (If you see a wider band, you are picking up the second one.) Keep you eyes unfocused and ask the person to breathe in and out deeply. Does the silver band change in any way?

Try seeing other people's auras several times with different people assisting you. Notice how the silver band changes for each one. Do you notice any other colors beyond this translucent or silvery band? Practice this activity several times a day for a few days—whenever you see a person standing against a

Once you are experienced seeing auras, you will be able to see another's aura by simply standing a few feet in front of him and staring with a soft focus. Having your partner stand in front of a white wall eliminates distracting backgrounds.

solid background—and you will almost certainly begin to see other, changing colored auras. The changing colors are often thought to be coming from a person's changing thoughts or feelings and are fun to observe. See if asking a person to think a loving thought—or a mean one—changes the colors you see.

Seeing Auras

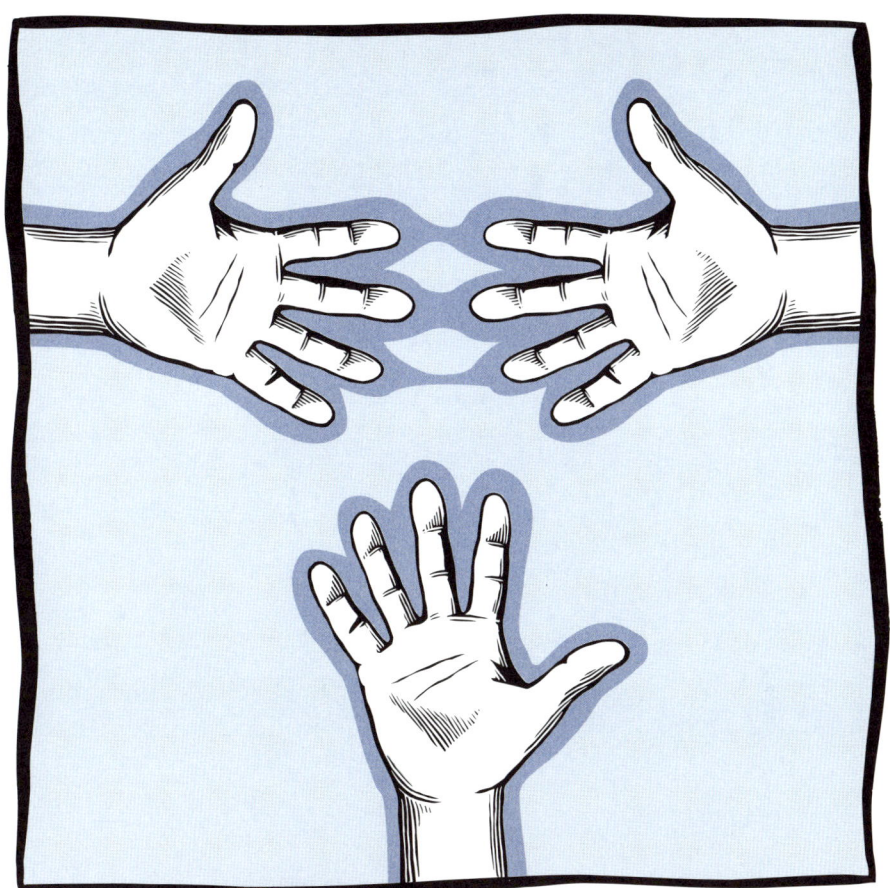

To see the energy surrounding your own body, try observing your hands, focussing the same way you do to see the aura of another person. You can see the aura around your own hand or even around the hands of your partner.

Now hold your hand at arm's length, and look at it with this soft focus. Can you see the same type of band around your hand? This is your own body aura.

Scientific explanations of this phenomenon—that the colored auras are created by reflected light or by the biomechanic functioning of our eyes—do not detract from the fact that there is more to see in the world than what we see at first glance.

You can also *feel* a person's aura. Have your partner stand facing away from you, several feet away. This time, instead of trying to see the aura, stretch your arms out in front of you. Push the air away from you, like you are pushing on an invisible swinging door. Then pull backward, as if you are letting the door come back toward you. Do this several times, slowly, really feeling the energy you are pushing forward and backward through space. Your partner should begin to sway, slowly, and ever so slightly, as a result of your motion. It's quite fascinating, given that he or she can't even see what you're doing since they're facing the other way! Take turns doing this to each other so you can both experience feeling and pushing energy that you can't see.

STRENGTHENING YOUR AURA

We know that a weak aura is usually caused by poor habits that destroy or weaken your different energy fields. The good news is that some simple adjustments to those habits can strengthen your aura. For instance, getting more sunlight, exercising, eating smaller, more frequent meals, playing soothing music, lighting a scented candle, or meditating regularly—even for just ten minutes a day—can all strengthen your aura.

To see how simple it can be to strengthen the aura, try the following. While you are looking at someone's aura, as you did in the earlier experiments, and when you feel you have a good view of it, ask the person to take a series of deep, cleansing breaths. For example, have your partner take a slow, deep breath in on the count of five, hold it for five, and release it for five. After a few of these breathing exercises, notice what's happened to the person's aura. Has it changed size? Usually, this cleansing will expand the aura. Have you ever noticed that when you get anxious or stressed out, or are straining with exertion, you often forget to breathe? Now you can see why this makes matters worse. Taking deep breaths can strengthen your aura and make you feel re-balanced within minutes.

The impact of positive thought on an aura is also impressive. At dowser's conferences, I've seen amazing examples of this. For instance, a person stands on a stage. An experienced dowser can dowse the aura (we'll learn how to do this in the next chapter). Once the dowser has located the outer edge of the person's second or third aura, the dowser turns to the audience and asks all of the people in the room to send loving thoughts toward the person. The dowsing instrument swings backward!

You can actually feel an aura's energy with your hands. Try sending appreciative thoughts to your subject and see if his aura changes in size or strength. What happens if you send disparaging thoughts?

The loving thoughts send energy toward a person and that makes the aura expand. Sometimes it can expand to have outer edges that reach outside the auditorium! So you can see how important it can be having a positive attitude yourself, and having positive, loving people around you.

Next time you come home from a long day at work, where everything went wrong, take a scented candle and go sit for just five minutes in a quiet room. Even if you have to lock yourself in the bathroom to do it! Light the candle. Stare at the flame and

KIRLIAN PHOTOGRAPHY

"I sing the body electric" is not just a metaphorical song lyric. Auras exist because our bodies are, in fact, electric. Still skeptical? Kirlian photography (also called electrophotography or corona discharge photography) is a special photographic method that captures the electric field around the body by using a high voltage machine that reacts with the body's electricity, producing what is called a corona discharge. This discharge is invisible to the naked eye in daylight, but can be seen in a dark room, and in the photograph. Some believe the glow around the object, particularly visible in photos of people or other living organisms, captured by Kirlian photography is a photo of the aura.

This technique was perfected in the 1940s by Semyon Kirlian, a Soviet electrician. The object being photographed is placed in a dark room on an unexposed sheet of film. The film is set on an electrode that is covered with a thin sheet of plastic or glass (a non-conductive material). What's to say this isn't just a physical representation of an electric field—not really an aura at all? This may be true, but what is probably happening is that the corona discharge visibility is being influenced by the energies in the aura as demonstrated below. Experimenters have demonstrated that the energy coming from plants or other subjects photographed in this way actually change when the physical or emotional states of the plant or subject are changed. For instance, Kirlian once spent all night photographing two identical-looking leaves someone had given him. He felt he was a failure because while one leaf photographed quite well, showing a healthy glow around it, he could barely get a faint glow to show up around the other leaf. When he revealed his dismal results the next day to the man who'd given him the leaves, the man was thrilled: one of the leaves had been taken from a healthy plant, the other, from a sick plant. The photographs did, in fact, represent the correct auras of the leaves!

notice the beautiful, soft, easily seen aura-like layers of the flame. Breathe in deeply. Let your mind wander. Try to think of nothing but the flame—not the work still sitting on your desk, not what you'll make for dinner. You can set an egg timer and promise yourself that just for five quick minutes you'll let your mind wander and replenish your energy. It's amazing how quickly you can go from feeling totally depleted to feeling re-energized. This is just a tiny, but effective example of how simple it can be to re-balance, re-energize, and strengthen the aura. Believe me, our body's energies are very responsive to proper attention.

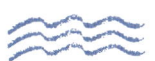

CHAPTER TWO

DOWSING

"Dowsing is a way to get in touch with your intuitive side. I like to think of it as a mother's intuition with a read-out device."

DOWSING

WHAT IS DOWSING?

Water witching, divining, questing, doodlebugging—all of these are terms you may have heard for dowsing. I like to think of dowsing as mother's intuition with a read-out device. It is a way for you to get in touch with your intuitive side, to tap in to your subconscious. The dowsing instrument that you use is simply a way for you to access these parts of yourself: you ask questions and your intuitive powers answer them the way you've "programmed" your subconscious to respond using the instrument of your choice, whether it's a body movement or the reaction of some dowsing tool.

Dowsing originated as the ancient art of searching for water, minerals, and other objects using a divining rod. They may not always admit it, but lots of people—even police departments—use dowsers to find lost objects, missing persons, or plane wrecks. Most farmers—and even the Marines—dowse for water. Today, more and more people dowse for fun, to heighten their intuition, strengthen their spirituality, to get in touch with earth energies and the environment, for guidance in personal decisions, even to help themselves lose weight, or otherwise improve their health and well-being.

How do you dowse? Dowsers project an "intent" or a "request" to an instrument to find the location of a specific object or target. There are many handheld instruments that serve as dowsing tools: L-rods, pendulums, bobbers, and Y-rods. These are all instruments that point the way, or answer questions that lead the way, to the object or answer being searched for. Most dowsers use all of these instruments, depending on which is handy or perhaps easier to use for specific jobs. Some come to prefer one instrument over another, or have better luck with, say, a pendulum, over a bobber. In your kit, we've provided you with two of the most popular instruments to use for your experiments: the L-rod and the pendulum.

HOW DOES DOWSING WORK?

We are all skeptics and want a rational explanation for how walking along with a simple tree branch in the shape of a Y can lead someone to the perfect spot to dig a well, or how holding a pendulum over a map can locate a lost plane. So I always like to introduce newcomers to the amazing world of dowsing with some research and theories about how dowsing might work. I find this helps people when they start out because, first of all, in order to get results, it's important to believe that dowsing can work. And having some understanding of how it might work usually helps beginners to believe. Also, it takes some of the "spook" out of it!

There have been many attempts to explain the often mind-boggling results that dowsers can get, but no single explanation has been agreed upon. Skeptics have suggested that when dowsers locate a precise spot to drill a well, they are responding to the physical terrain of a place without realizing it, instinctively knowing where water will be found beneath the ground based on clues from the land above. Some believe that it must be an external force that guides the instruments, rather than an internal force that emanates from the person dowsing. But this doesn't explain why some dowsers don't need an instrument, they just tune in to physiological changes they feel in their body when they dowse, and let these changes guide them.

The most likely explanation is that dowsing is the ability to tune in to some force that science has not yet identified. For instance, water and the items that dowsers find may have a natural magnetic, electromagnetic, or other unknown energy to which dowsers are able to attune their instruments. A fairly simple science experiment shows how moving water can cause electricity to flow. Water drops moving down a wire will rake off enough electrons to cause a small neon bulb to flash—a requirement of over 68 volts. (You experience something similar when you slide across a plastic seat and get an electric shock when you touch someone.) Water flowing underground also causes some kind of electric current. Any time electricity flows in any kind of conductor, it creates an electromagnetic field. What if this field could then be picked up by internal sensors that we all have?

Is it possible that we have sensory systems that enable the brain to pick up mental processes that we are not consciously aware of? Back in 1983, a neurophysiologist at the V.A. Medical Center in Loma Linda, California, reported observing effects from electric fields only one-millionth as strong as those formerly considered threshold levels in humans. This was news to most scientists, but not to many dowsers! Dowsers have frequently conducted experiments at dowsing conventions in which they passed electricity through ground, and found they could easily pick up the resulting electromagnetic energies. Scientists have identified three sensors that can pick up this electromagnetic information. One is near or in the pituitary gland (in the brain), and there is one on each adrenal gland (near each kidney). The theory is that by comparing the information from these three internal sensory points, the brain can determine both the distance and direction of an electromagnetic source without our conscious awareness—much in the way the brain uses the two eyes to calculate how far away an object is, another thing the brain does without us consciously thinking about it.

So how do we get this sensory information from the unconscious to our conscious mind? That is where dowsing comes in—in particular, the dowsing instrument. Experiments have been performed in muscle testing, in which the subconscious can be programmed to cause involuntary muscles to be strong for a true statement and weak for a false statement. There have also been experiments that test the muscles in dowsers, with the finding that dowsers move their instruments with involuntary muscle movements. Do you see how this could work? Say our internal sensory systems pick up electrical currents from the flow of water underground. Our conscious mind may not "know" we feel these electrical signals, but the sensory systems could trigger involuntary muscle responses that indicate the "yes" response in dowsing instruments. The muscles of the body respond involuntarily, guided by the unconscious—or at least, by that of which we are not aware.

Perhaps you're saying, "But that doesn't explain map dowsing or information dowsing." After all, dowsers are able to locate things by dowsing a map with a pendulum; and they are able to dowse for this information by "programming" their subconscious to respond by giving certain signals indicating a "yes" or "no" to questions. (You'll learn to do this later.) What kind of energy could our internal sensors be tuning in to in these instances?

Map dowsing seems to be related to something called the "Backster Effect." Cleve Backster is a lie detector specialist who attached a galvanic skin response detector (a lie detector, in effect) to the top leaf of a plant. This device measures the electrical resistance of the skin—or in this case, the leaf. He then watered the plant, intending to measure the amount of time it would take for the water to reach the leaf and change its electrical resistance. To his surprise, the detector immediately indicated a response that correlated with a "happy" response in humans (the galvanic skin response that equates with a happy state). Puzzled, he decided to measure a traumatic response in the plant by burning a leaf. The plant showed a fear response on the lie detector *as soon as he had the thought*. He hadn't even picked up the match yet! (Ever notice that people who talk to their plants have the best green thumbs?)

Backster's experiments have been duplicated thousands of times, using many variations, by many scientists. These experiments and others like them have been argued to show that there is some type of energy—I'll call it "superconscious energy," for lack of a better term—that seems to have been flowing through Backster's mind and the plant. Have you ever felt ill at ease or apprehensive for no apparent reason? Perhaps this is the undetected energy that explains a mother's intuition.

A basic theory is, then, that using a dowsing instrument

allows your subconscious to tap in to the wealth of information available from this superconscious energy. It follows, therefore, that water dowsing is the most physical type of dowsing because it is most closely related to your body's own sensitivity to the electrical currents of underground water. Dowsing for objects is also likely related to the body's allowing itself to tune in to electrical currents. It seems more psychic in nature, however, because you really have to let your rational mind let go of preconceptions in order to get in touch with energies you are not conscious of.

WHO CAN DOWSE?

According to the American Society of Dowsers, everyone is born with the ability to dowse. Of course, much like learning to play an instrument, you can't just roll out of bed and start doing it perfectly. It takes practice and dedication to become expert at dowsing. And like any talent, some of us are born with more innate ability than others. Children, in fact, are more sensitive to dowsing up until the age of about fifteen—perhaps because they have not yet developed a mindset against the idea. Some adults will find that they have a gift for dowsing almost immediately, but most have to practice to hone the skill. I've found that when you first try dowsing as an adult, about 80 to 85 percent of us can eventually acquire the skill.

I first dowsed for water when I was twelve years old. I enjoyed dowsing for years, but when I went to college and studied science, I figured dowsing wasn't going to be looked upon too kindly, so I stopped. Many years later, teaching science at the college level, I woke up one day frustrated at how narrow my world had become. I decided to take up dowsing again and it opened my world right up. For many people dowsing is a way to break out of a mold, to begin to tune in to your immediate world and the circumstances around you, and to exercise your right brain, especially if you're caught up in a left brain career.

GETTING STARTED

Hopefully, by trying some of the exercises in this book, you will discover the fun of this ancient art. But before you begin trying out the different instruments, some preparation work will increase your chances of early success. Find a quiet place, a comfortable spot where you can be alone—if only for a few minutes—each day. When you're first starting out, it's ideal if you can go to this spot at about the same time each day. It can be as simple as sitting up in bed at night, or at your kitchen table or desk in the morning. Once you have learned to dowse, it is less important that this be a predetermined place and time. But when you are getting started, it can be helpful. It is like making an appointment with your subconscious, or taking a few moments to get in touch with your spiritual beliefs. Just become quiet, and let yourself drift into a relaxed state.

The two most important factors in dowsing are faith and relaxation. If you believe you can dowse, you will have much more success than if you come to these experiments full of doubt. And being in a relaxed state allows you to let go of your conscious mind and let the subliminal forces in your body lead the way.

Once you're adept at this, the fun begins: trying out the instruments.

THE INSTRUMENTS

Dowsing instruments provide the "read-out" to whatever force it is that dowsers access. Whether that force is the unconscious, "mother's intuition," or an energy that science has yet to identify, we don't know. But I can tell you the energies are there to be found, you just need to learn to tune in. If you work at it, and learn to trust the instrument and the results, you will be amazed. Let's review the basic instruments.

L-Rods

Also known as an angle rod, swing rod, or pointing rod, the L-rod is one of the most popular dowsing instruments because it is so easy to make and use. Of course, you won't have to make your own, because we have provided two in your kit. But just in case you find yourself needing to fashion one on the fly, it's good to know how. Usually made of wire, it is simple to fashion an L-rod out of a coat hanger. A welding rod is also a popular material choice, but you can use just about anything you can bend into an L shape. The top wire of the L can be anywhere from four inches to over two feet long, though twelve to sixteen inches is a standard length.

You can use one L rod alone, or use two together. When one is used, hold the rod loosely in your hand with the top wire tilting slightly downward. The rod acts as a pointer or a swing rod. It can be requested to point toward a target or direction, or to swing sideways when encountering a specific energy field (such as an aura or a noxious zone). If you are using two L-rods, they are normally programmed to point straight forward for the ready position, to cross over each other for the "yes" response or when over a target, and to swing outward for the "no" response.

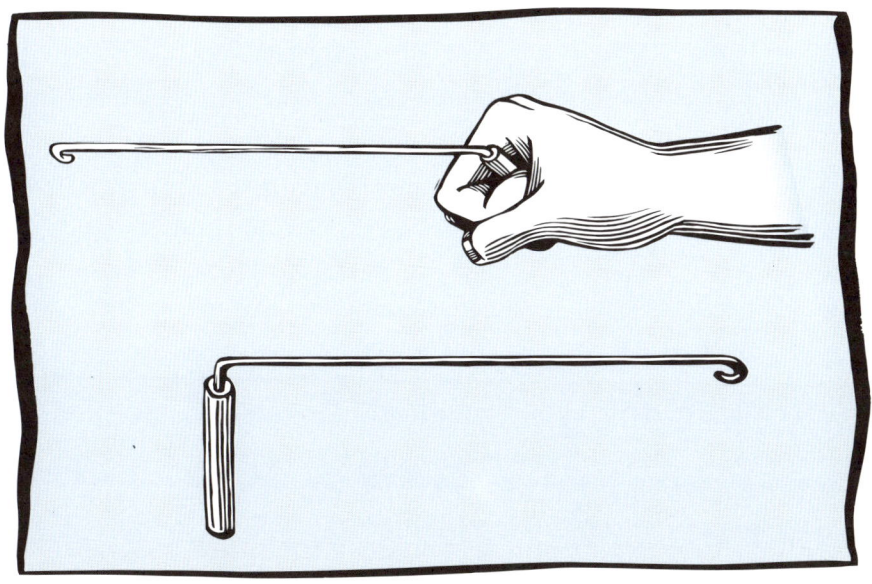

The L-rod is one of the most popular divining instruments. Hold the short handle loosely, with a comfortable grip, and let the long wire point slightly downward.

You can make your own pendulum out of a favorite talisman: a cross, ring, pendulum, cork, or crystal. Just hang it securely and evenly from a chain or even a string. Sometimes a person might feel most comfortable working with an instrument of his own making, with an object of special, personal significance.

THE PENDULUM

In your kit you'll find a traditional pendulum on a chain. But a pendulum can be anything that you hang on a string or a chain—from a paper clip hanging on a thread, to a favorite rock or talisman hanging on a jewelry chain. You can use anything; some people like to follow their instincts for what will work best for them. The pendulum is one of the most popular instruments because it is easy to make and use. It is small enough to go in your pocket or purse, and it is excellent for dowsing maps and charts.

The pendulum is used with "yes" and "no" questions. The string is held between your thumb and forefinger, suspended so that it dangles about three to four inches. The usual responses you program your dowsing system for the pendulum are: swing straight forward for a "yes" response; swing sideways for "no"; and swing at an angle when it is "ready for question." You can program your dowsing system for the pendulum to respond any

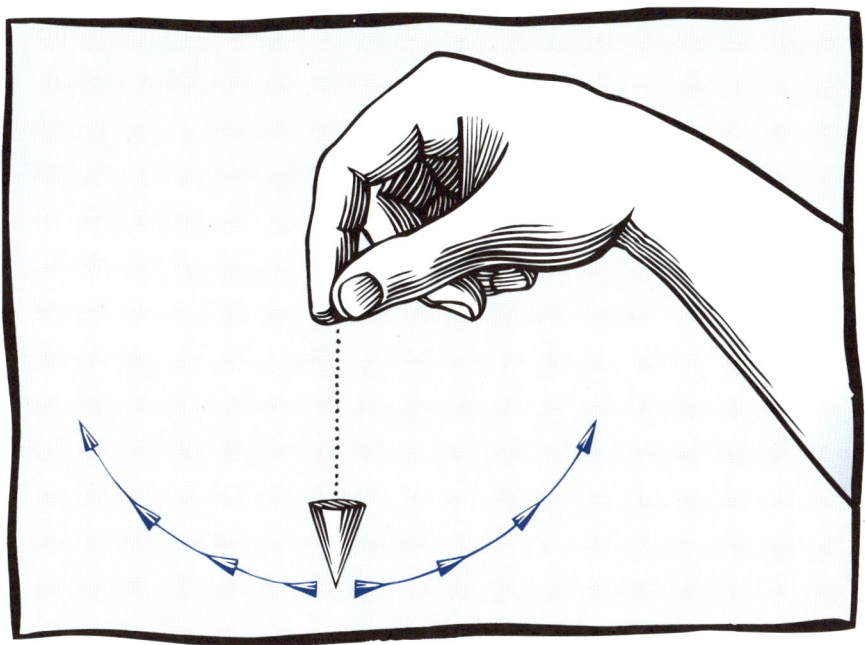

You must program your pendulum to swing in one direction in response to the "yes" questions and another direction in response to the "no" questions you ask it. You can choose the direction you prefer for the responses.

way you like, however. For instance, since using a pendulum in the wind or while walking can disrupt the direction of swinging, under these circumstances programming it to spin clockwise as a response to "yes" and counterclockwise as a response to "no" often works better.

THE BOBBER

The bobber (also called the wand, spring rod, or divining rod) is any flexible, long thin rod. It tends to be anywhere from one to four feet long. You can fashion a bobber out of a thin tree branch, stripped of leaves and shoots, a piece of stiff wire, or any flexible pole. Some modern ones have a coiled wire and a weighted tip.

The bobber is held with one hand pointing down at about forty-five degrees. You can program your system for the bobber to act like a pendulum, with bobbing up and down for the "yes," or swinging side to side for the "no." You can also program the bobber to give different responses, such as swinging back and

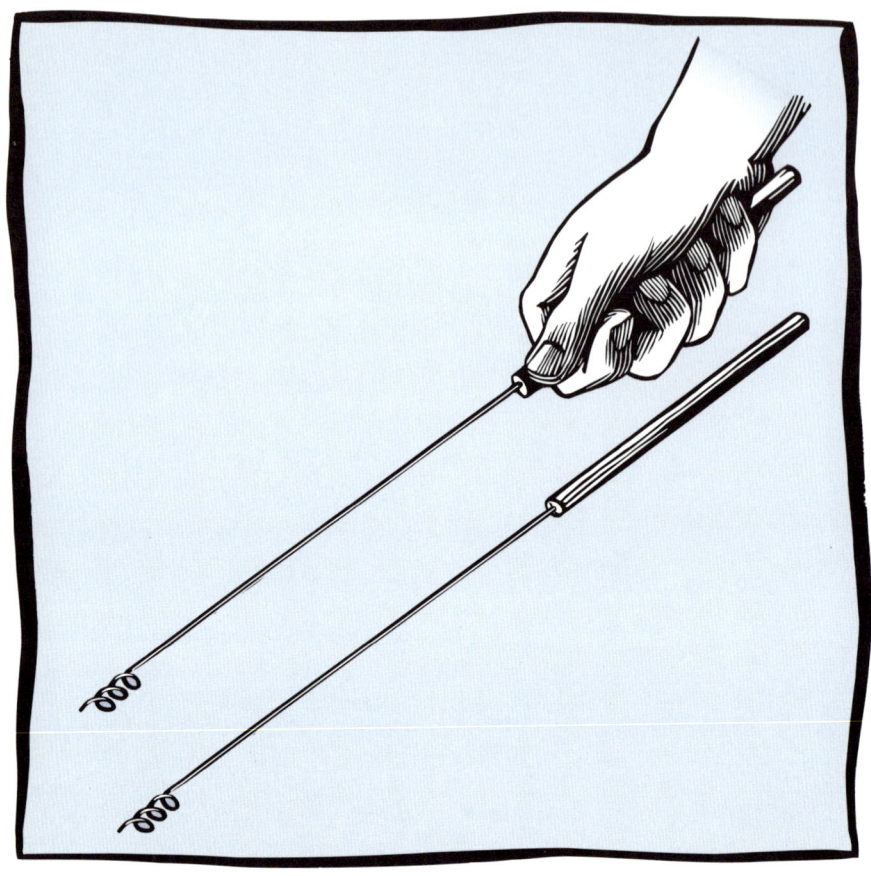

The bobber is often used in the field to substitute for a pendulum which has the same motions. It is generally pointed down at about a 45° angle.

forth toward the target you've requested, and spinning when over the target.

Most dowsers find this an easy instrument to use, and it often replaces a pendulum for field work. Unfortunately, it won't fit easily in your pocket or purse, so it's not good for those who want to be able to dowse at a moment's notice!

THE Y-ROD

The Y-rod, forked stick, or talking stick, is perhaps the oldest dowsing instrument. It can be any size, but is usually about 12 to 24 inches long and about 1/8 to 1/4 inch in diameter. The Y-shaped rod can be wood, metal, or plastic. It is fun to make one from a tree branch, the way the ancients did. Today, many dowsers use plastic Y-rods (probably for the ease of storage), and they work just as well.

To use the Y-rod, you begin by holding each branch of the Y, palms facing up, with the end pointed down. Rotate your palms outward until the Y-rod swings up. Typically programming for the Y-rod is: pointing upward at about forty-five degrees is the "ready" position; swinging down from the ready position is the "yes" position; swinging up from the ready position usually means a "no" response.

One advantage of the Y-rod is that it is quick: it can point directly to a water vein or target. It also works particularly well if you are walking over rough ground, and is reliable even in fairly strong winds. However, it is not as versatile as other dowsing tools since it has only the up and down motion. You need to turn your body to find direction.

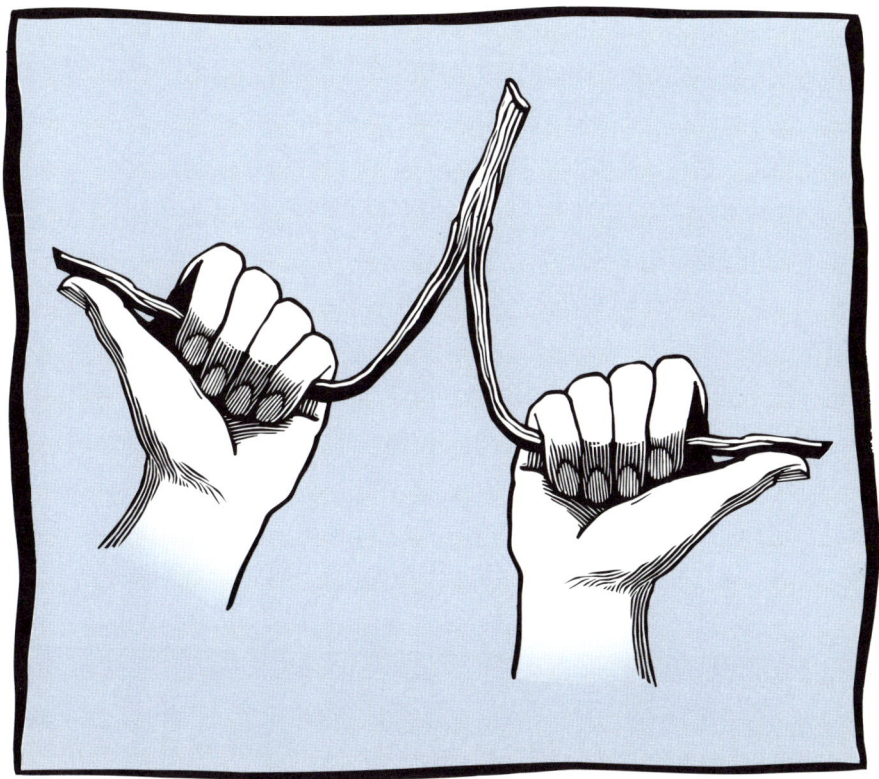

The Y-rod is the classic dowsing instrument for "waterwitching." Purists love making it from a tree branch, the way the ancients did. It is held, palms facing up, with the end pointing away from you. Typical programming is "Ready": 45° up; "yes": pointing down; "no": swinging upward.

PROGRAMMING YOUR DOWSING SYSTEM

What is this "programming" I've been referring to? Learning to drive a car, swim, write—these are all programs. They are skills we learn, we are not born knowing how to do these things. But once we learn these skills, they become second nature; we don't have to constantly think about how to write our name, we just pick up a pen and do it. We have to program ourselves to be able to use dowsing instruments too.

If dowsing instruments are ways of communicating, then it makes sense that in order to communicate clearly, you have to know what messages your instruments are sending you, right? For instance, you have to know if your pendulum is swinging straight up and down it's saying "yes," or if it's swinging to the side it's saying "no." So you have to program your dowsing system. Some people get confused and think "programming your dowsing system" means you're teaching the pendulum or the L-rod to do certain things. This isn't true. YOU are your dowsing system. You program yourself so that your subconscious, or intuition, or whatever energy it is we're tapping in to, can trigger the correct response in the instrument you are using. Once you've "installed" a program, meaning once you've trained your dowsing system to respond in certain ways with a pendulum, for instance, you're done. You don't have to install a new program each time you use a different pendulum. You don't have to teach yourself to write your name again when you pick up a new pen, do you?

If you are interested in pursuing dowsing further when you finish this book, you'll see that as you get more advanced, the language for programming can seem a bit unwieldy at times—almost sounding like a legal contract. This is because it is very easy for language to be imprecise, and precision is the key to successful dowsing—as we'll see in this next section!

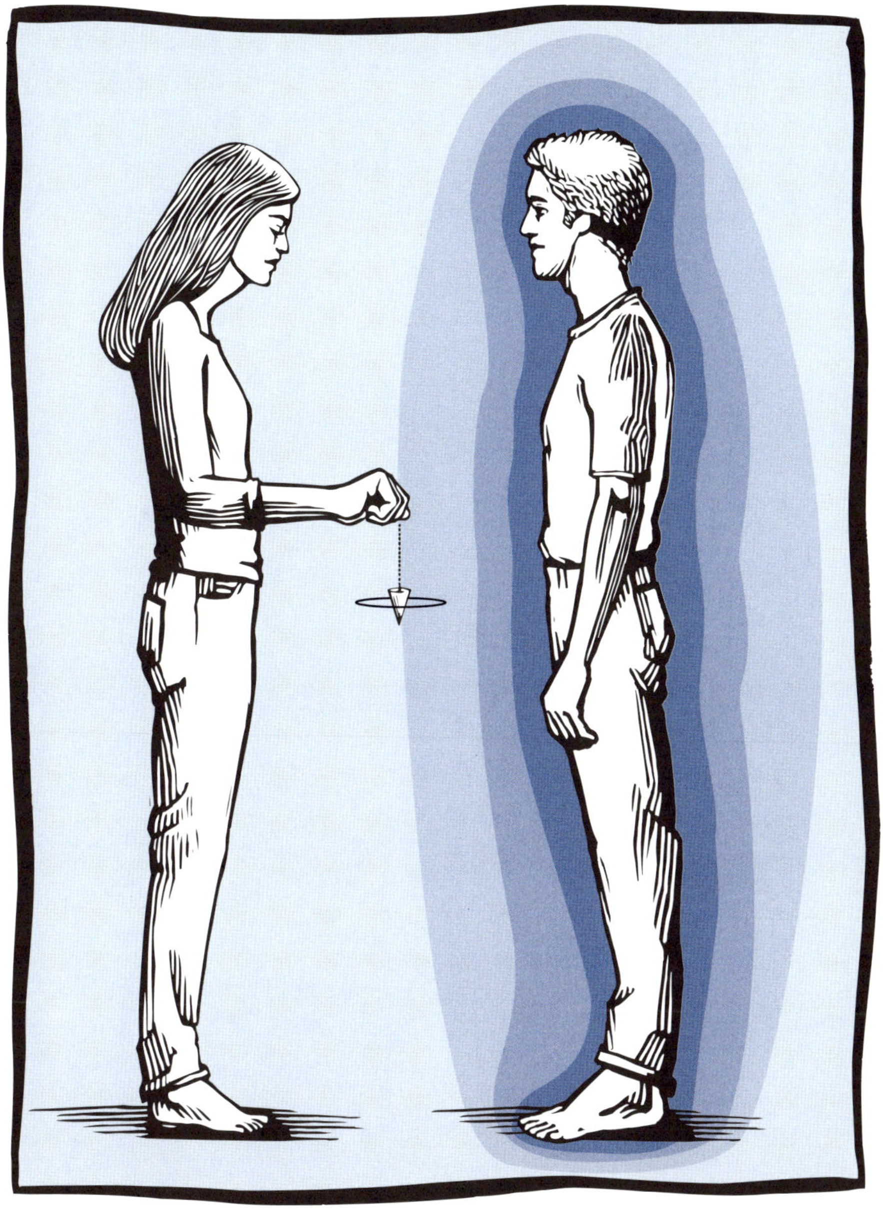

When using the pendulum to dowse another person's aura, walk towards the subject and ask the pendulum to spin in a particular direction when it reaches the outer edge of the subject's aura.

THE QUESTION

The wording of the question you ask is probably the most important part of dowsing. There was a story in the American Society of Dowser's journal about an experienced dowser who was leading an instruction course. He asked his L-rod to point to North. But rather than point north, the rod swung straight out and pointed to the audience. This was strange, he had never had this problem before. He tried again. Again the rod swung out to point toward the audience. The dowser began discussing some possible reasons for this erroneous response when a hand went up in the audience. "My name is North," said the man.

So you can see, the response was correct for the question posed. In this case, the question should have been, "Point to the earth's magnetic north" in order to achieve the correct response. Another example would be a question like, "Does my car need gas?" At first glance, this seems to be a simple and obvious question. But the answer would always be "yes" even if the tank were full: a car always needs gas in order to run. The dowsing system takes words and phrases literally. If there is a conflict or ambiguity in your question, you may not get the clear results you are seeking. Just as if, with the programming, if you are not in agreement with your dowsing system about what every word means, and what every response indicates, your answers may not be accurate. When posing a question always:

1. Be specific about what you want to know. Include what, where, and when instructions in the question.

2. Use only words, phrases, and conditions whose meanings are not ambiguous. (You may not always realize they are ambiguous, like in the North example, so be careful!)

3. Make sure you have programmed an agreed-upon method of response from the dowsing system you are using, so that you don't get confused responses. For instance, make sure you've programmed your L-rods to cross for a "yes" response if using two, but to point in a certain direction for "yes" if you're only using one. Otherwise, you could find you're using one L-rod and it may still be swinging in the direction it would to cross for a "yes" response as if you were using two, and that response may therefore not really mean "yes."

4. Make the question a definite request for information that actually exists. Avoid asking for an opinion. If the question does involve an opinion such as, "Do I have enough money?" then make sure you make it specific using the what, when, and where qualifiers mentioned above. For instance: "Do I have enough money, in my pocket, right now, for a two-dollar ice cream cone?"

Consider these rules when applied to the question "Am I strong?" for example. Your answer is based on what you think is meant by the word *strong*. A person can be physically, mentally, or emotionally strong, to name just a few obvious interpretations. So the question must be refined. Add indicators of what, where, and when: "Am I strong enough to pick up this one gallon carton of milk, right now?" That is how specific you need to be.

You can see how tricky it can be to formulate a good question. And how you can easily set off on the wrong path if you don't realize you've started with an imprecise question. If you are specific, you save yourself time and prevent yourself from getting off track.

So how do you know if your question is a good one? If you are good at the game "twenty questions" you will be good at formulating good dowsing questions. The best way to begin is to ask multiple questions to hone in on specific results. For instance, say you are dowsing for water to drill a well in a certain area and you begin by asking: "Is there water in this area?" The answer will be "yes" because there is water everywhere. So the more precise question you should ask is, "Is there a water source, less than three hundred feet deep, that could supply five gallons per minute?" (the amount you need to drill a well). Again, the answer is "yes," because this could be true during a severe rain storm. A further question may help you zero in on the correct answer: "Could this water source allow a well to supply five gallons per minute of potable water to the surface, year round?" If the answer is "no," you know your first questions weren't specific enough, but you've saved yourself the time of dowsing for a water source that will not provide the needed results.

Another good way to assure accuracy with important questions is to check out your results with an experienced dowser. Have another person ask the question in their own way. If you get the same results, you will be reassured. If, however, the results are different, you should both reexamine your questions. Remember, the question can be the key factor in accurate dowsing.

You will find that it becomes fun to examine language this way and realize how much of what we say is open to interpretation if it is taken literally. Don't let yourself get frustrated or perfectionistic. Dowsing is meant to be fun and relaxing. It is a way to open yourself up to intuition and flow. If you tense up and become overly serious or concerned, this will hinder your results. Look at forming the question as a word game—it is, in many ways like "twenty questions." The more you practice, the better you'll get. Allow yourself to play and enjoy it.

Now that you understand dowsing and the prep work, let's program your dowsing system for the instruments in your kit and start dowsing!

CHAPTER THREE

DOWSING WITH L-RODS

"One thing you should know about dowsing is that the dowsing system does not like to play games. So be careful with 'testing.'"

DOWSING WITH L-RODS

Even though the Y-rod was the original dowsing instrument, today most people begin dowsing using L-rods. They're easy to program and use, and many get results right away. Take the two L-rods in your kit. Let's begin with the correct way to hold them. Stand straight with your palms clasping the shorter end of the rods, so that the longer sides are pointing straight ahead—kind of like a cowboy holding a couple of six-shooters. Hold the L-rods so they are pointing down ever so slightly.

L-rods held in the "ready" position.

I'm going to give you the traditional way to program them for "yes," "no," and "ready (or waiting)" responses. You can program different responses later on, if you like. Tell the L-rods you want them to cross. Say it out loud once, and then focus your mental energy on making the L-rods cross. They should slowly move into the crossed position. Tell the L-rods you want this to be the "yes" response.

Now tell the L-rods you want them to go back to pointing straight ahead. When they get there, tell them you want this to be the "ready, or waiting" position. Now tell them to swing out to point away from each other. When they do, tell them this is the "no" response. Now practice several times, to make sure the dowsing system is programmed. Ask the L-rods to show you the "yes" response, and wait for the L-rods to cross; then ask them to show you the "no" response. They may move slowly at first, until your responses build up confidence with practice. For some people, the L-rods swing quickly into place. It all depends on your personal energy levels.

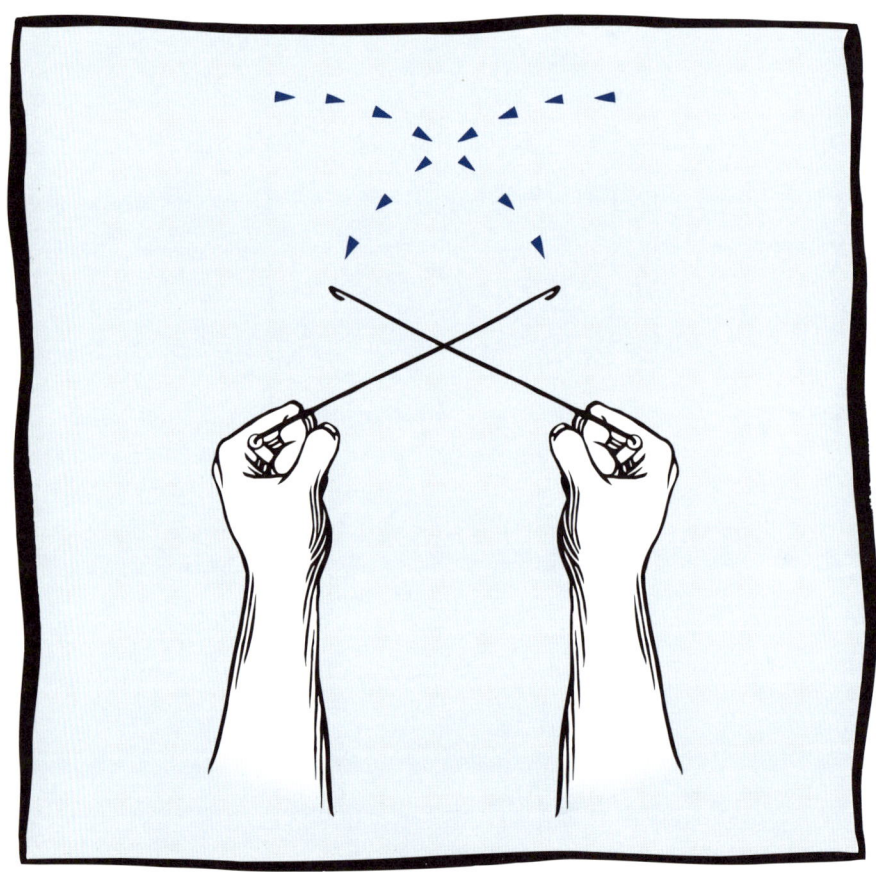

L-rods crossed in response to programming, usually for a "yes" response.

Dowsing with L-Rods

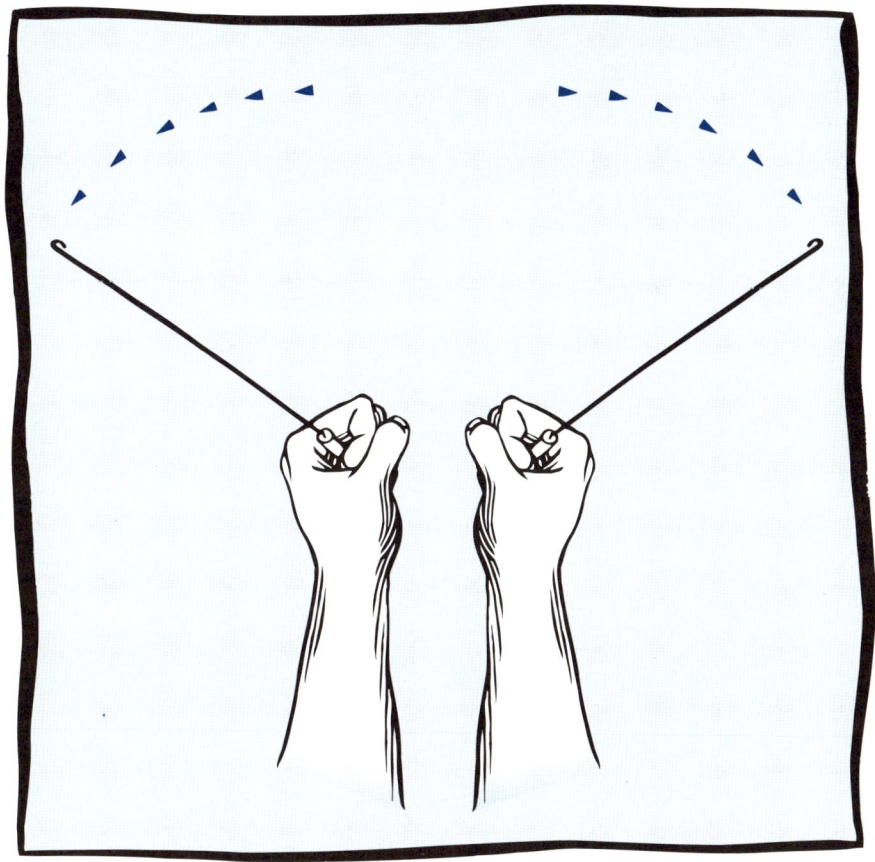

L-rods in the open position, usually programmed as a "no" response.

ASKING FOR PERMISSION OR GUIDANCE

Once you're happy with the responses, you're ready to begin dowsing. You can start with some simple "yes/no" questions, or with searching for objects. However, one thing you should know about dowsing, is that the dowsing system does not like to play games. So be careful with "testing" it. Especially early on, this can be harmful. It's easy to get wrong responses when you are starting out—like anything, it takes practice to do it right most of the time. So if you test the system and get a wrong response, it can shut down your intuition. For this reason, I always urge people to ask permission from the system to "practice" when you start out with simple exercises or questions. This way you limit the doubts and mistrust.

In fact, the first step in dowsing for *anything* is always to ask for permission or guidance. Most dowsers do this by prefacing each dowsing session with the question: "May I, Can I, Should I dowse for [the name of what it is they're dowsing for]?" In order to ask this question, you have to make sure you and your dowsing system agree on the meaning of this question. So whenever you are first programming your dowsing system, you should read this mini-program out loud, to install it:

"**May I, Can I, Should I Program** is to become a working part of all my dowsing programs and be continually in effect until I choose to make changes. When used in reference to dowsing questions, May I, Can I, Should I is to have the following meaning:

May I means: Do I have appropriate permission?

Can I means: Do I have the ability to successfully dowse in this area, and am I ready?

Should I means: Considering all aspects related to this situation, would it be appropriate, proper, and suitable to dowse in this area?

End of program. Thank you."

Now, with your L-rods in the "ready" position, ask out loud: "May I, Can I, Should I practice with some 'yes/no' questions?" If the response is "yes," begin. If it swings to "no," try again later.

Assuming you got a "yes" response, try some of these questions—and any others of your own. It's best—and most fun—to ask these questions of someone about whom you don't know all the answers already.

Yes/No Practice Questions

- Are you older than thirty? (Keep asking questions until you hone in on the age.)
- Do you have brown eyes? (blue?, hazel, etc.)
- Do you own a car?
- Are you married?

- Do you have children?
- Do you have one child? (more than one? two? three, etc.?)
- Do you play a musical instrument? (piano?, violin?, guitar, etc.?)
- Do you have any siblings? (brothers? sisters? one? two, etc.?)
- Do you like your job?

Check your results after you've gone through a series of questions, rather than after each question. This way you don't disrupt the flow or your confidence as you practice! And don't be discouraged if you dowse an incorrect answer. Even the most experienced dowsers sometimes miss a correct answer, often because of the way they worded the question. With practice, you'll get better and better.

FINDING A LOST OBJECT

Finding lost objects is definitely one of the most fun—and most practical—kinds of dowsing. It's also what convinces people that dowsing works. It's important to be specific about what you're looking for, and to trust the results you get.

Say you can't find your house keys. Begin by asking, "May I, Can I, Should I dowse for my lost keys?" When you've gotten permission, ask if the system is aware of the object you are looking for: "Are you aware of my keys to open this house?" If the system says "yes," you can ask, "Can you find the keys?" Always ask this first: if the system CAN find the object. It may not be able to because of numerous reasons. Then ask, "Can you lead me to the keys?" If the answer is "yes," then ask the system to point the rods in the direction you should go. Are they in the house? in the living room? the kitchen? Hone in on the room or general area with "yes/no" questions. Then ask the L-rods: "Please point the way and cross when you reach the spot."

It's a good idea to begin each new dowsing session (whatever the instrument) by asking for permission or guidance with the "Can I, May I, Should I?" question.

Remember, you can program the dowsing system for the rods to do whatever you want them to. You may want to use just one L-rod to lead the way, and ask it to swing out, or spin around when it reaches the destination.

A friend and fellow dowser had a situation where he had

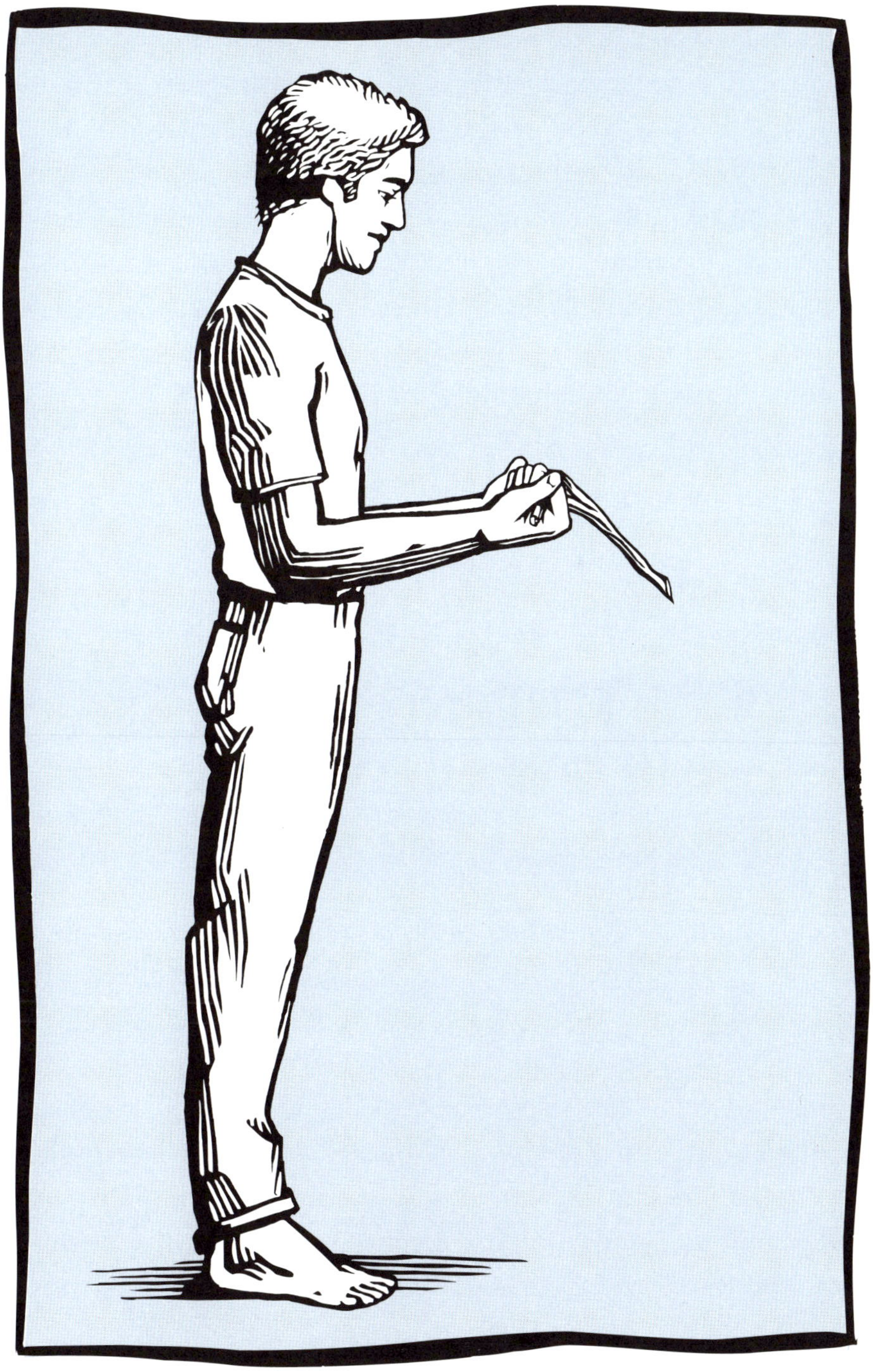

Dowsing with L-Rods

When your dowsing system finds a lost object, it will indicate a "yes" response. In this case the Y-rod dips down to point out the object, or indicate a "yes" response.

lost his airline tickets. He was in the living room of his home. He asked his L-rods if they could locate the tickets. The answer was "yes." So he asked them to point in the right direction. They led him into the bedroom and crossed right over his dresser. He went through every drawer but couldn't find the tickets anywhere. He asked again if the tickets were in the dresser and the system insisted the answer was "yes." So he searched again: still, nothing. He started over, from the front of the house, and again the L-rods led him to the same spot. After the third time, he gave up. Then he thought about it and went back and looked more thoughtfully at the dresser. He bent down and peered underneath the dresser. It turned out the tickets had been on top of the dresser, and they had fallen off and been swept underneath. There they were: exactly under the dresser.

To practice searching for objects, you can have a friend hide an object for you. But remember, be sure to tell the system you are practicing, and get permission to practice.

FINDING THE FLOW OF WATER

I mentioned that I started dowsing when I was twelve years old by looking for water. It wasn't just a game, it was a necessity. I went to a one-room schoolhouse. For water, the teacher used to bring a bucket of water with a ladle and we each had a cup. That was all we got. We lived a day's travel from another village. With no electricity, no phone, no radio, and no internet we had to depend on social activities. So during the Depression, the neighbors got together and built a grange hall. This was a huge success: there would be seventy-five people at a meeting, from babies to great grandmothers. But again, water was a problem. There was only one barrel of water brought on a pickup truck. So the grangers decided to try to dig a well. They used three dowsers from the grange group to dowse for a water vein. They thought that their Y-rods had to be from a willow branch picked on the north side of a bush, picked in the morning, and that it couldn't be used for more than a day because it would dry out. Each dowser set out with his Y-rod and independently agreed that there was one spot where they should dig for a vein of water thirty feet below the ground that would provide a well.

One of those dowsers was my father. I picked up one of those sticks and tried it, and it pointed straight down at the same spot!

The grangers got together and began digging through hard clay. After several weeks, they were at 29 feet. The hole was still bone dry and folks were worried. But they kept digging. But at 29 1/2 feet they hit moist clay. So they took a shovel and carefully cut the veins in half and took a mirror to shine sunlight down into the hole so we could all take a look: there it was, water, thirty feet down.

Here's how you can get that same thrill I got from seeing that water bubble in the very spot the dowsers had identified.

To practice, it's simplest to begin by looking for a known water source. (I've not met many people who want to go to the trouble of actually drilling a well to see if they're right.) This can be done by dowsing for a well on your own property, or at a neighbor's. Or you can try looking for a water pipe that goes into your house.

Here's how to dowse for the well on your property, assuming you don't know where it is. Go outside your house and stand with your L-rods in the ready position. Ask your L-rods, "May I, Can I, Should I dowse for the well that supplies water to my house?" When you've gotten permission, I suggest you use just one of your L-rods and ask the dowsing system to point the way to the well. Walk in the direction the rod is pointing. Ask the rod to swing out when it comes to the well. Once you find the spot, you can also dowse to find out how deep the well is. Take both L-rods and ask them to go to the "ready" position. Ask "Is this well more than ten feet, twenty feet, etc.," until you hone in on the answer.

If you know the location of the well on your property, you might want to dowse for a water pipe that goes into your house, instead. Or for spots at which the water veins lead into and flow out of the well.

Experienced dowsers can go to a barren piece of land and use their instruments to locate the exact spot a well should be drilled. To dowse for water for a well, you need three pieces of information: the location, direction, and depth of a water vein. Water flows underground through veins that can twist, turn, and branch off into different directions. Veins run through sand, gravel, and bedrock cracks, and tend to flow over or under clay (not through it). Veins can be a few inches to many feet wide and can give off anywhere from a dribble to much more than ten gallons a minute. So the proper question is very important when dowsing for water for wells. A good complete question would be: "Is there a water source [indicate the size of the area you wish to check] that is less than three hundred feet deep and will bring water to the surface from a well at a rate of more than three gallons per minute, that is potable and palatable and in a legal spot?" If the answer is "yes," then ask your dowsing tool to lead you to the best spot to drill a well.

If you are serious about this sort of dowsing—or any kind, for that matter—it can be helpful when you are first starting to have an experienced dowser with you. Going to a dowsing club meeting is an excellent way to get started with dowsing, and is a lot of fun. The American Society of Dowsers (802-684-3417) can let you know the locations of meetings in your area.

DOWSING THE AURA

Your aura is constantly changing according to your attitude—whether you're frightened, or feel good, or if someone's sending love signals (or hate signals) to you. It can be hard to develop the skill to see all three of its layers. Dowsing the aura can help you to see how far layers that are harder to see extend. You can also identify weak areas by dowsing.

Have a friend stand about six feet across from you. First, take both L-rods and ask, "May I, Can I, Should I dowse this person's aura?" It's especially important to ask for permission when dowsing other people. If you get a "yes," then I recommend dowsing the aura with one L-rod. Take the L-rod and hold it in the "search" position. When dowsing for the aura, the easiest way to start is to ask to locate the average of the first three layers, or specify the first, second, or third auras, whichever you prefer. Ask the L-rod to swing out when it comes to your chosen aura level. Now walk slowly toward your partner. When the instrument begins to swing outward, you are at the edge of the person's aura. You can ask a person to think loving thoughts, and start over. This should make the aura expand.

You can also dowse individual parts of the body to determine the shape of the aura, or to determine ailments. For instance, if a person has a bad knee, and you are using L-rods, the rods might cross in this area.

You can dowse someone's aura to determine how far out the aura extends, or whether it is strong or weak, or how it responds to positive or negative thoughts.

Ley Lines and Earth Powers

If you have ever had the good fortune to visit an ancient monument such as Stonehenge or Avebury in England, you probably noticed that the place made you feel calm and serene. Perhaps you attributed this to its awesome history. But did you ever consider that the reason the place evokes such reverence might have to do with the earth's energies?

Many ancient monuments happen to have been built upon spots where the earth's energies—water and ley lines—come together to form power centers. Ley lines are part of the earth's energy system that carry positive energies. They are cosmic forces that penetrate and leave the earth vertically. Water lines often carry a negative charge. The nodes at which ley lines penetrate the earth are called power centers. These power centers have domes, where water lines rise up through the earth, where they meet the positive and negative energies and are usually in balance. A fascinating and eerie discovery was made by Alfred Watkins, who noticed that if you were to connect them on maps many ancient monuments are aligned on straight lines. Could the ancients who built these monuments have been tuning in to these powers? Many believe these spots are the sacred sites on which monuments like Stonehenge, or the pyramids, were built, because the balanced energy created such a sense of well-being in those who visited these places.

Like water veins, ley lines can be dowsed. Once again, though these mysterious earth energies cannot be seen, dowsers can tune in to their power.

FENG SHUI

Feng shui is the Chinese "art of harmonious placement." The Chinese believe it is important to carefully seek out the best places for humans to live in harmony with the earth and universe.

Life energy, or *chi*, is the most important aspect of feng shui. The Chinese believe everything is composed of chi and that this energy must flow freely through us and our environment for good health. For centuries they have held that to have a harmonious life, we must maintain a balance—within and around us—of the chi, the flow of cosmic energy. Could this chi be the equivalent of the electric energy we have been discussing? Feng shui provides tools to read the landscape and improve one's well-being by redirecting and balancing chi.

The rules of good chi also happen to make good design sense—for instance, getting rid of clutter or arranging rooms to let energy flow. Dowsing can help you determine the flow of chi in your home. You can dowse the flow of chi, and identify where it may be blocked in your home, or a room. Using your L-rods, stand at the door to a room. Ask your L-rods, "Show me the flow of chi." The L-rods should turn into the chi stream (see figure).

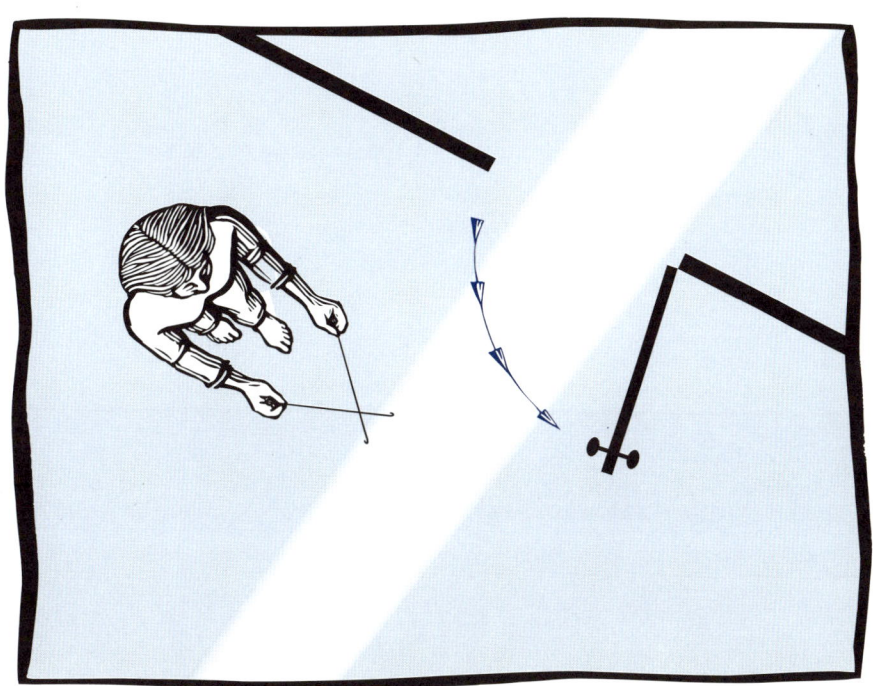

CHAPTER FOUR

PENDULUM DOWSING

"Dowsing can open up your world, and help you get in touch with creativity and intuition you didn't know you had—or hadn't trusted before."

PENDULUM DOWSING

All dowsing is dowsing for information, in my view. But people may sometimes differentiate one type of dowsing from another. The kind of dowsing we did in the last chapter—such as dowsing for a spot to drill a water well—is often called "on-site dowsing." Dowsing for something using a map—or from the edge of a property—by asking questions can be called "off-site dowsing." And for many, dowsing for the answers to questions is considered "dowsing for information." Most people's favorite instrument for this kind of dowsing is the pendulum. For instance, you can use a pendulum to help determine the right place to plant your garden, to identify correct health habits, even to help you lose weight! But first, let's program your dowsing system for how you wish to have the pendulum respond.

PROGRAMMING YOUR PENDULUM

Working with the pendulum, I find it is especially important to be in the relaxed state I talked about practicing in chapter 2. So if possible, you might want to try this and go back to your favorite spot at your regular time. Let yourself drift into that prayerful, alpha state.

Once you feel calm, you're ready to begin. Take your pendulum and hold the string or chain between your thumb and first finger. Hold it with about two to three inches of string length. (Notice that the string length determines how fast the pendulum will swing.) Hold the pendulum over the center of the "Yes/No/Ready" chart we've provided below.

Moving your hands and fingers, manually start the pendulum swinging in the "yes" direction over the chart. Ask and expect the pendulum to keep swinging on its own, without your help. Ask this out loud, in the same tone and loudness as if you were talking to a person: "Keep swinging in the 'yes' direction, without my help." If the pendulum stops swinging, start it again, and repeat the request, like you did with the L-rods. Keep watch on only the upper, or forward, half of the pendulum's swing, ignoring the other half of the arc (from the center toward you). Repeat this process until the pendulum continues to swing on its own.

Now do the same thing for the "no" direction on the chart. Keep your fingers over the center of the circle on the chart and continue to ignore the same half of the pendulum's arc-shaped swing. Once the pendulum is swinging by itself in the "no" direction, ask it, while it is swinging, to work its way clockwise back to the "yes" direction. Then ask it to continue to the "ready

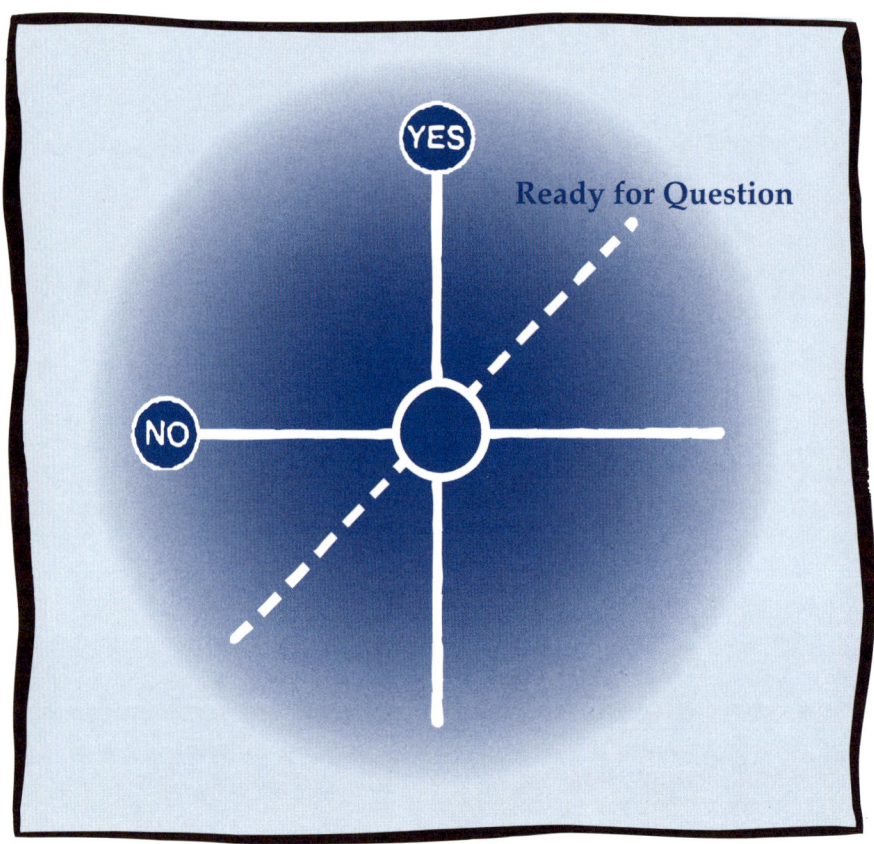

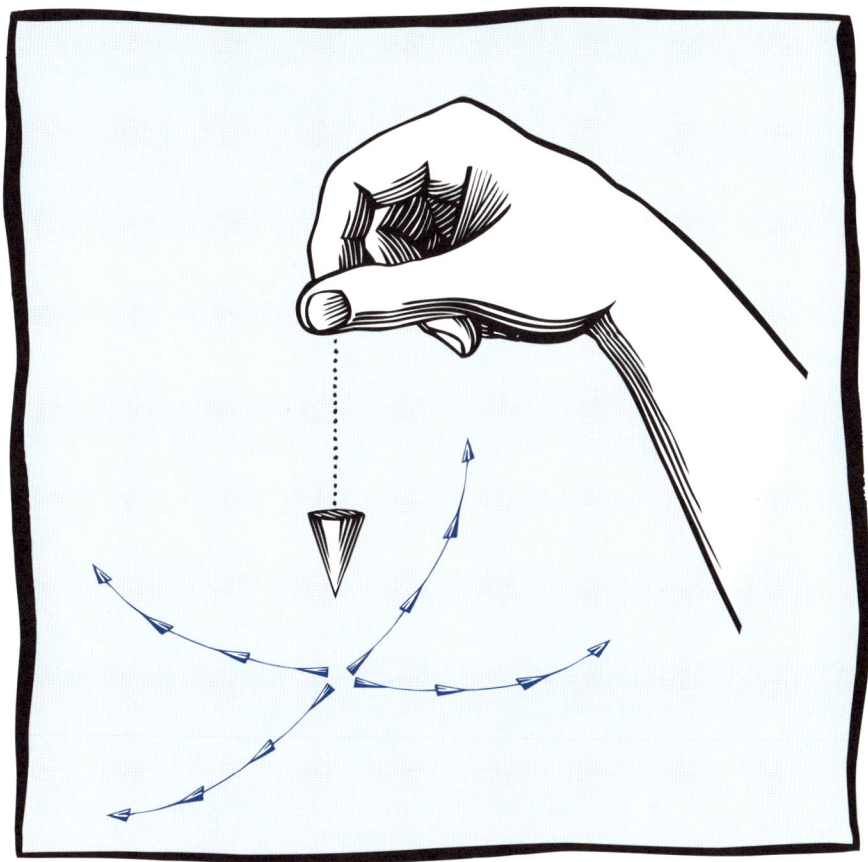

Program your pendulum to swing in a forward direction to indicate a "yes" response, and in a sideways direction to indicate a "no" response. Many dowsers prefer the pendulum because it is so portable; it slips easily into a pocket for transport. You need never be without it, which can often come in handy!

for question" direction. One the pendulum has done this, ask it to work its way counterclockwise: from the "ready for question" direction, to "yes," and then to "no." Then ask it to go back on a clockwise path, back to "yes." Practice this several times.

If you cannot master this simple program within about fifteen minutes, take a break and try again later. You may be experiencing interference, which is common when you are starting out. But don't give up. Keep trying.

This is the most basic program for a pendulum that allows you to ask "yes" and "no" questions. This will give you a good start. But you should know that there are other basic programs you should install in your dowsing system if you want to do some serious dowsing.

DOWSING FOR INFORMATION

With your system properly programmed to use a pendulum, and if it is responding well, you can now ask some practice questions. Remember, the first step is always to obtain permission. This is true with any instrument you use. With your pendulum swinging to the "ready" direction, ask it, out loud: "May I, Can I, Should I practice with some 'yes/no' questions?" If the pendulum swings to "yes," you're ready to begin. If it swings to "no," try again later.

Say you have a garden in your yard, and you've bought new plants but you're not sure where to put them. You can dowse for answers. Go into your garden, and take your pendulum and the "yes/no" chart. Ask "May I, Can I, Should I dowse for the correct positions for my new plants?" It's likely the answer will be "yes."

You can ask a number of other questions to help your planting. For example, "Would [describe the location] be the best place for [name of plant] to maximize its health and vitality?" If the answer is "yes," you should get digging. If the answer is "no," you can do one of two things. Either position the plant in other spots and ask the dowsing system if any of these might be better, or just keep asking the system about different locations, without actually moving the plant. Once you've found a good spot, you can then ask the dowsing system what is the best position for the plant. For instance, turn it so that one side is facing the sun and ask if this is the best position. Twist it around until you can get the "yes" response. You can also ask questions about how often to water certain plants, about whether they need plant food or fertilizer, or whether certain pesticides would help or hurt. Always be specific, and always frame the question so that the answer is an objective "yes" or "no."

Some people find pendulum dowsing can help with losing weight or quitting smoking. I think it is the power of focusing your mental energies on these problems that makes this so effective. Take your pendulum and ask, "Can you help me lose weight?" If the pendulum says "yes," then ask permission to dowse for this first. Then, close your eyes and get the image of the way you want to look in your mind's eye. Maybe it's an old photo of yourself before you gained weight. Focus on that image of yourself as the goal. Ask the pendulum: "Can I weigh this much again?" If it says "yes," you might ask, "Can you help me to not overeat and only eat the foods I need to stay healthy, and to exercise?" It will likely say "yes." Then you can ask how long this will take to achieve: "A year? six months? four months?" until you pinpoint an answer.

Here are other examples of questions you can ask to dowse for information.

HEALTH
- Is this form of exercise (name it) beneficial to me?
- Am I getting all the vitamins and minerals I need?
- Do I need to take a supplement?
- Am I getting enough sleep?
- Is this food good for me?

RELATIONSHIPS
- * Is this a good relationship for me?
- Should I date this person?
- Does this person respect me?
- Can I trust this person?

DOWSING FOR NOXIOUS ZONES

I believe that one of the most important functions of dowsing is dowsing for noxious zones, also known as geopathic zones. These are energy zones that result from various earth energies that can be harmful in large doses. The interesting thing about noxious zones is that they may not be harmful until they hit a certain level. Below that level they actually stimulate your defense systems and may be beneficial. Also, the level that's harmful is different for each person. It's like jogging. Jogging is

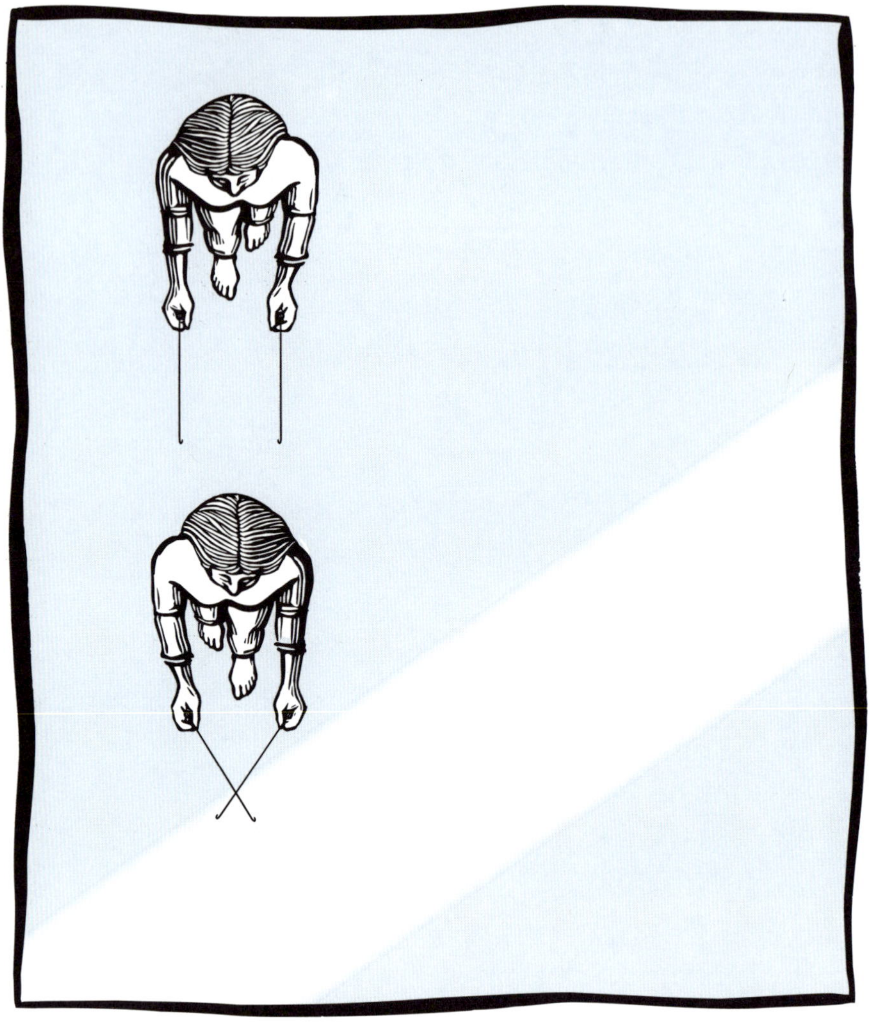

Dowse to determine if and where there are noxious zones in your home or office, and ask how much exposure is too much for you, or someone else. Then you can alter your environment or habits accordingly.

good for you up to a point. But if you overdo it, it starts to be harmful. This is how noxious zones work. The trick is to determine, 1) where they are, and 2) how much exposure is too much for a particular individual.

Many people who have trouble sleeping, or who have recurrent illnesses, often discover that their bed, for instance, is over a noxious zone. Maybe they can only take about four hours of that noxious zone until it becomes harmful, but their spouse is fine for up to eight hours—which explains why the spouse exhibits no troubles.

Dowsing for a noxious zone is simple. Simply ask your pendulum: "Are there any noxious zones in my home?" If the pendulum says "yes," start narrowing down the rooms or areas where they might be. Once you've narrowed it down to a room, say it's your office, then stand at the door of the room with your pendulum. Ask the pendulum to spin clockwise when you come to the noxious zone. Start walking across the room in a straight line. Walk the room like a grid until you've located the noxious zone area with your spinning pendulum. (You could also use your L-rods in a similar way.) Perhaps it's right near your desk where you work all day. Now ask the pendulum, "Can you tell me the detrimental level of this noxious zone for me?" If the answer is "yes," start asking, "Is it more than eight hours? seven hours?" etc., until you pinpoint the level. To fix the situation, you can either move your desk so that it's not over the noxious zone, or move whatever needs to be rearranged so that you're not exposed to the zone more than for the detrimental time level. There are also ways to remedy this with a more advanced use of the pendulum and a more complex chart. To learn more, see "Letter to Robin," Walter Woods's guide to pendulum dowsing (available from the American Society of Dowsers).

READING MAPS WITH A PENDULUM

Map dowsing is a way to search for something by using a map or chart. This is often done when whatever is lost could be anywhere over a huge distance and it's simply impractical to dowse for it in person, or perhaps the terrain is too dangerous to dowse on site. For instance, it's often done when searching for plane wrecks or missing persons.

A common method involves using a map, a marking device (such as a straight-edge ruler) and a dowsing instrument (usually a pendulum), and the "yes/no" chart. Begin by carefully describing the missing person or thing and asking permission to dowse for it. Then ask if the dowsing system can find the lost thing or person. If it says "yes," ask it to indicate the target as you

Use a ruler and your pendulum to dowse over an appropriately detailed map or chart for lost objects, pets, or people. This method is particularly useful when the area to be searched is too large or treacherous to do so by foot. Searchers for plane wrecks or missing persons frequently use this process. You can dowse directly over the map or chart or over a "yes/no" chart like the simple one we have provided on page 68.

begin to slide a straight-edge ruler across the map or a drawing of the area, from left to right. Now, with your pendulum over the "ready for question" or "yes/no" chart, ask your pendulum to indicate "yes" when the straight-edge is at the target. When the pendulum swings in the "yes" direction, stop moving the ruler and draw a line along the edge. Now turn your edge ninety degrees and slide it from the bottom, toward the top of the map. Again, ask the pendulum to indicate when the straight edge is at the target. When it indicates "yes," draw another line along the straight edge. Where the lines intersect is the target area.

You can also dowse a map by asking your pendulum to swing in the direction of the target you are searching for. Slowly move the pendulum in the direction it is swinging and ask it to spin when it hits the target.

Dowsers have had amazing success with this. I was once part of a group that was asked by a group of archaeologists to dowse a map of a Native American burial ground for the body of the "most important person" from this tribe. We dowsed the map and indicated a spot they should dig, three feet below the surface. Within ten days we received word that they had dug at the spot we indicated and found what appeared to be the remains of the chief, surrounded as he was by important artifacts.

A FINAL WORD: BE WARY

Dowsing can open up your world, and help you get in touch with creativity and intuition you didn't know you had—or hadn't trusted before. But I do want to offer some words of caution. When sensing for information, DO NOT attach yourself to it. By this I mean treat the questions and the results objectively, don't try to tune in to or feel the results. The advantage of using a dowsing device is that you do not have to physically sense or become a part of the energy you are dowsing. This is especially important when dealing with unhealthy or noxious energies.

A helpful way to avoid absorbing undesirable energies is to simply program or direct your mind to have a detached sensing attitude. Talk to your pendulum or dowsing instrument as if it were a person. This will direct the energies to the instrument, not you. This keeps your mind on the action of the instrument, and not on the energies themselves.

Dowsing is fun and can be helpful to yourself and others. But it is a skill that should not be pushed too far or abused. Be wary of overstepping your bounds. Here are some issues to always respect:

PERMISSION OR GUIDANCE: The reason it is always important to ask permission when installing a program, or before dowsing, is that you never want to interfere with anyone else's "lessons in life," or their "karma," or other unknown areas.

So if the answer to "May I, Can I, or Should I" is ever "no," then you should tactfully avoid or decline to pursue a subject further.

There seems to be a universal law of cause and effect (the idea that you reap what you sow), known as karma. To maintain good karma, always dowse for the good of others. Remember, learning to dowse well is a gift. It should never be used for evil or selfish gain. It is fine to dowse for your own needs, or the needs of others. Always treat your dowsing skills as a gift to cherish for yourself and to give to others.

PRIVACY: Never dowse a person without their permission, or personal request. Tuning in to the subconscious provides access to lots of information. It is like reading someone's diary without their knowledge.

DIAGNOSING: DO NOT diagnose or give medical advice of any kind. If, in dowsing someone, you suspect they have a problem, urge them to seek medical advice. Note that under the U.S. Federal Pure Food, Drug, and Cosmetic Act of 1976, it is a violation of the law to attempt, in any way, to diagnose or treat any ailment or illness unless you are a medical doctor or other licensed health-care professional working under the most stringent State, AMA, and FDA approved conditions. Use good judgment, be cautious.

SHARING YOUR ABILITIES WITH OTHERS: As with any unexplained ability, dowsing may frighten or offend some people. Be discreet with your new skill, sharing it with those who want to know or who may be open to it, but keeping it from those who will look on it unkindly or with fear.

Finally, always keep an open mind to new ideas and look for ways to improve your skills. Being a lifelong student of dowsing can bring much joy and excitement to you and your friends. Try not to let your beliefs or preconceptions block you from examining new ideas. Keeping it simple is the most effective way to dowse. Keep practicing, but most of all, keep enjoying!

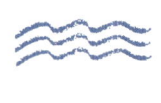

CHAPTER FIVE

CHAKRAS

"Many people believe that human energy zones emanate from the center of an individual in a wheel or lotus-flower shape."

CHAKRAS

Chakras are another way we can tap in to creativity and intuition. The Sanskrit word *chakra* means "wheel." In India and other cultures throughout the world, many people believe that human energy zones emanate from the center of an individual in a wheel or lotus-flower shape.

According to Indian spiritual beliefs, there are over 88,000 chakras, on just about every point of the human body. Most of these are very small points; there are only about forty significant secondary chakras. But when people work with balancing the chakras, they are usually working with the seven major chakras. It's believed that these are the main energy points on our body that energy flows in, out, and through. They are located at the base of the spine, the reproductive center, the solar plexus, the heart, the throat, the brow, and the crown of the head. Each of the chakras is associated with symbols and sounds—and a particular color of the rainbow.

CHAKRAS AND THE AURA

Many people believe that the colors of our human auras are related to the strength of these energy zones, or chakras, of the body. Since the chakras are the points at which we take in and give off energy, they impact the size, color, and strength of the aura. For instance, the ethereal body is believed to draw energy from the sun via the solar plexus chakra and to draw energy from the earth via the root chakra. The ethereal body stores and transmits this energy to the other chakras. It seems reasonable to imagine that the ability to take in and store good energy is important to good health, since the ethereal body is responsible for physical health. If you have a strong ethereal or body aura, you can repel illness. If it is weak, you are susceptible to illness.

The astral body is responsible for our emotions and is the next aura layer, as you may recall. Any changes in emotion radiate out from the astral body via the chakras. The belief in India and many other countries is that the energy we send out attracts the same kind of energy that we take in. Therefore, if we subconsciously harbor fears or anger or unresolved emotions, we are likely to attract the very situations or people we most want to avoid! Have you ever experienced this? Say you are someone who is afraid of confrontation, yet time and again you find yourself in situations with people who are provoking you. Why is this? Because you have not unblocked or resolved this energy within yourself! Thus you keep sending it out and attracting it. The idea is that by identifying these blocks, we can accept them, feel the pain behind them, and then cleanse them from our systems, replacing the negative energy with positive energy and freeing us for unconditional joy and fulfilment.

The two other aural bodies that receive energy from the chakras are the mental and spiritual bodies. The mental body is responsible for our thoughts and intellect. It can provide linear thought form, or if it is connected to the spiritual body, it can tap in to a wealth of insights and intuition. Finally, the spiritual body (or causative body as it is sometimes known) is our connection to the creative life force. When this body is highly energized we are very connected to our true purpose in life and each chakra level can find its highest level of expression.

We'll show you some exercises to start identifying weak spots in your chakras, and one way to begin balancing them. It's worth a try, isn't it? As I like to say, nothing ventured, nothing gained! But first, let's look at each of the seven main chakras.

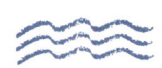

THE SEVEN CHAKRAS

ROOT OR BASE CHAKRA

The first chakra is the root, or base chakra. It is located at the base of the spine and is associated with the earth element. This chakra is related to the physical world—meaning both the material world and the physical well-being of our bodies. When this chakra is in balance you feel stable, rooted in your sense of self and in your life, and connected with nature or your surroundings. If this chakra is out of balance you can become preoccupied with material possessions, and with your own desires, and the result can be anger and violence; physically, you can experience constipation.

SACRAL OR NAVEL CHAKRA

The second chakra is the sacral or navel chakra. This chakra is located in the lower abdomen or navel area. It is associated with emotions, sexuality, creativity, and giving and receiving in cooperation with others. When this chakra is balanced you are aligned with others, open with your emotions, and in tune with creative energy and actions. When it is out of balance, the results can be jealousy, sexual problems, or, physically, low back pain.

SOLAR PLEXUS CHAKRA

The third chakra is the solar plexus chakra. It is located between the navel and the chest. As mentioned, this chakra is connected to the sun (it's the way the ethereal body gets its sun energy). It is associated with your power center. It's the place from which you radiate emotional energy to the rest of the

Colors of the Chakras

The seven major chakras are located at the base of the spine, the reproductive center, the solar plexus, the heart, the throat, the brow, and the crown of the head. Each is associated with a color of the rainbow. There are numerous interpretations for the different colors of the chakras. If you can develop your vision to the point where you can begin to see colored auras, think about the significance of the color that each person is emanating.

- *The first, or* base, *chakra, is associated with red, symbolizing physicality.*

- *The second, or* sacral, *chakra, is associated with orange, symbolizing vitality.*

- *The third, or* solar plexus, *chakra, is associated with yellow, symbolizing personal will.*

- *The fourth, or* heart, *chakra, is associated with green, symbolizing compassion and unconditional love.*

- *The fifth, or* throat, *chakra, is associated with blue, symbolizing communication.*

- *The sixth chakra, or* third eye, *is associated with indigo, symbolizing wisdom.*

- *The seventh, or* crown, *chakra, is associated with violet, symbolizing heightened consciousness.*

Chakras

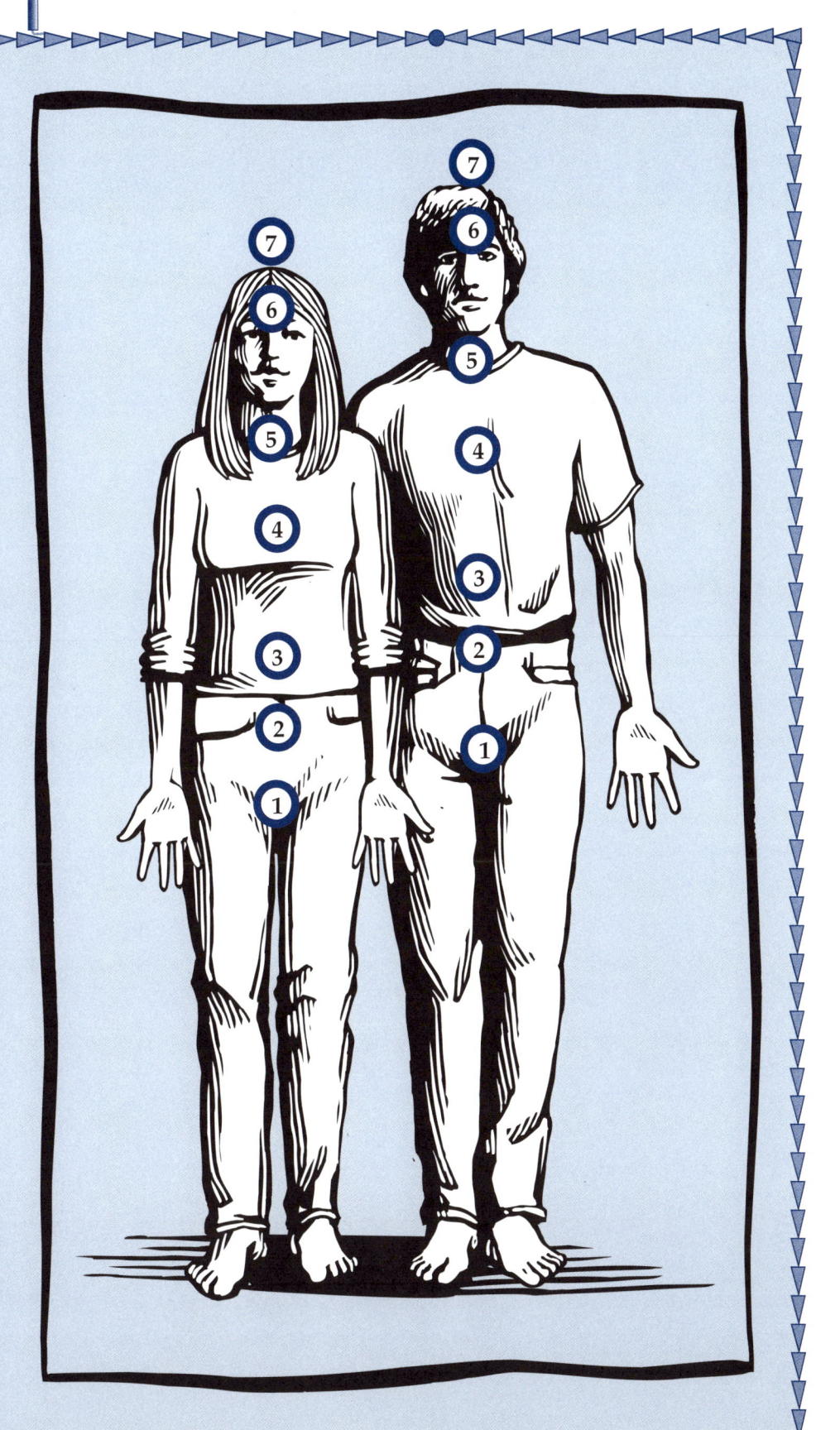

world. So when this chakra is powerful and balanced, you approach the world and others from a strong place. You have self-acceptance, harmony with your surroundings, and the strength to resist negative energy and attract the energy and people that will help fulfill your desires. If it is out of balance, you can experience a lack of will, fear of new challenges, trouble coping, anger, hate, blocked desires, and physically, may suffer from eating disorders or problems with digestion.

HEART CHAKRA

The heart chakra is fourth, and is located in the center of your chest. It is associated, not surprisingly, with love. Because it is at the center of the seven major chakras, it connects the lower chakras with the upper chakras. A completely open and balanced heart chakra can lead to unconditional love—of yourself, and others—that can be inspiring to the world around you. The compassion, love, and warmth radiated can bring joy and open others up. This can be a divine or spiritual form of love in its highest form. Imbalance in this chakra can be manifest in someone who gives away love, but has trouble receiving it, or who gives, but expects something in return. This can result in anger, lack of love, coldness, depression or, physically, heart troubles.

THROAT CHAKRA

The fifth chakra is the throat chakra and is located in the throat area. It is associated with communication. This includes all forms of communication: verbal, written, artistic, etc. Balance and strength in this chakra can result in the ability to honestly communicate about your feelings, to accept everything about yourself—the good and the bad—and be able to share this understanding with others. It can make you a good listener. And just as important as saying "yes" to requests, when this chakra is balanced, you can say "no" when that is in your best interest (or the best interest of others). Imbalance in this chakra can lead to lots of problems with miscommunication. For instance, with a weak throat chakra you may have trouble acknowledging your feelings to yourself and others. This can lead to a build-up of frustration and pain that go unexpressed. Or it might make it hard for you to talk to your boss or spouse about feelings or needs. This can make you tend to manipulate others, instead of asking for what you want. Other signs of throat chakra imbalances can include speech problems, ignorance, insensitivity, depression, and physically, throat or thyroid problems.

Brow or Third Eye Chakra

The sixth chakra is the brow or third eye chakra. It is located in the center of the forehead and is associated with wisdom and intuition. When this is balanced people experience active mental abilities and intellectual skills. Ironically, if this chakra is well developed these rational mind skills can be transcended, and intuition and imagination become stronger and develop into clairvoyance. This chakra, out of balance, can result in trouble concentrating—or perhaps a tendency to overanalyze things all the time. It can also lead to arrogance (thinking you know more than others, or that only things that can be "proven" with a certain set of rules can be true) as well as vision problems.

Crown Chakra

The seventh chakra is the crown chakra, located at the very top of the head. This is associated with spiritual or divine consciousness. There are believed to be no blockages that occur in this chakra; instead, it is developed to various degrees. The more developed this chakra, the more open you are to being in tune with a divine or creative force. If this is poorly developed, you can feel disconnected from a creative force, depressed, or uninspired.

TESTING THE CHAKRAS

So how do we know if our chakras are in balance or not? It is pretty difficult to read your own chakras, but here is an exercise you can do with someone else to test each other's chakras using dowsing. First, have your partner lay down on a table or the floor. Take your pendulum, and ask, "Can I, May I, Should I check [name of person]'s chakras?" If the answer is "yes," you may continue. Let's begin by finding each chakra. You can do this by holding your pendulum above the person and slowly moving it along their center line from just above the knees, to above the head. Ask the pendulum to spin when it comes to the edge of each chakra, beginning with the root chakra. When the pendulum spins as you approach the root chakra, you can ask,

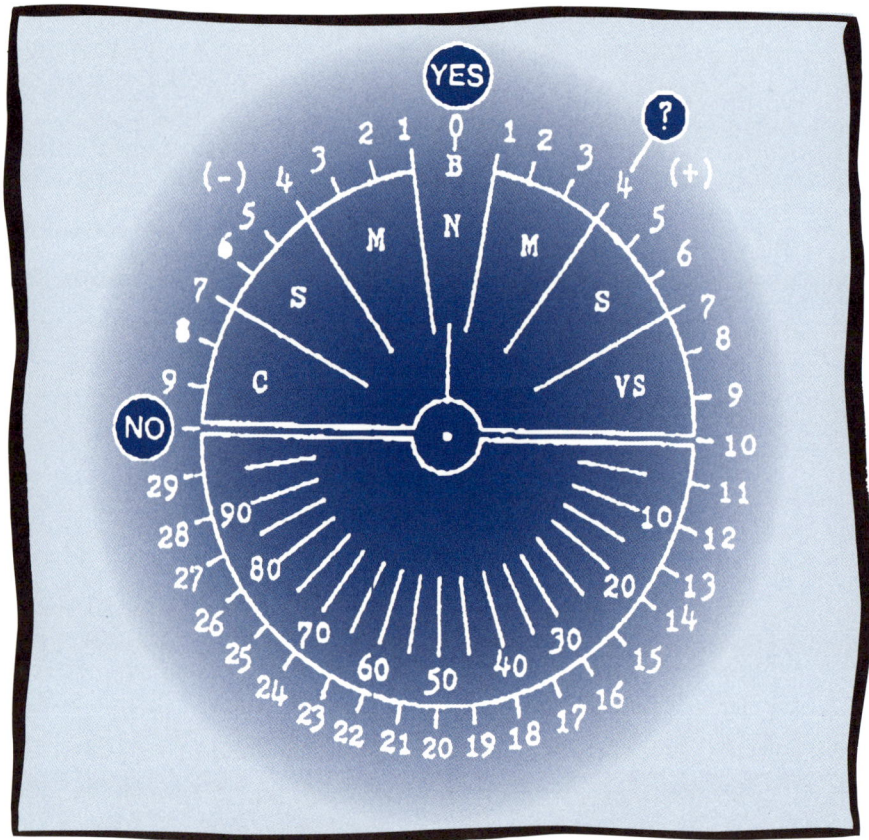

The chart above reads as follows: B = Balanced, N = Normal, M = Mild, S = Severe/Strong, VS = Very Strong, C = Critical.
(-) = Loss, Decrease, Less than, or Deficiency. (+) = Excess, Improved, Increase, or Surplus.
Numbers: May be % Degrees, Amounts, etc.

CHAKRAS

"Is this root chakra balanced? Swing up and down for 'yes,' or sideways for 'no'" (or whatever program you prefer).

Once you have done this for each chakra you will know which, if any, need balancing.

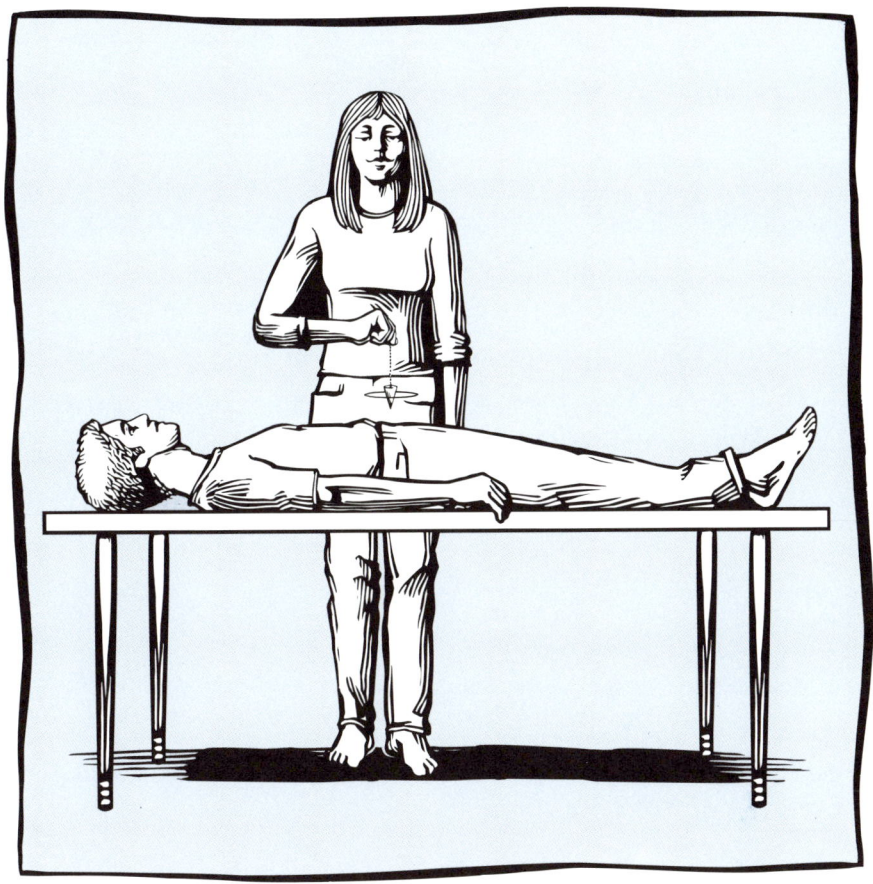

Use your pendulum to locate each of the seven chakras on a person. You can test for strength and health of each chakra by asking the pendulum if it is balanced. If the answer is "no," ask the dowsing system to balance each of them.

BALANCING THE CHAKRAS

There are many ways people balance chakras. Yoga or core energetic exercises may be used to open up different chakras—unblocking them and getting the energy moving through. Some people use color therapy, meditation, breathing, aroma therapy, even sound therapy. I like to use my handy pendulum.

If you've done the above exercise, you know which chakras need balancing. You can also ask the person to stand across from you several feet, and using the more advanced chart we've provided (opposite), ask the pendulum: "Are this person's chakras balanced?" If the answer is "yes," you're done! If the answer is "no," I would ask the system if the system can balance the chakras. If it says "yes," I would use the chart we've included on page 68 to ask the system: "What level are the chakras at now?" The pendulum should swing to indicate a point on the chart, probably on the negative side. While it is swinging over that number (say it is 4), I would ask, "Please bring the person to balance." The pendulum will work its way over to balance on the chart. If the pendulum says "no" when you ask if it can balance the person's chakras, then, again, you're done. There are reasons we don't always understand for why the dowsing system might say "no." Perhaps the person needs to do this for him or herself because there's a lesson or skill they need to learn that we shouldn't interfere with. You must always respect the answers you get.

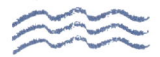

CHAPTER SIX

LABYRINTHS

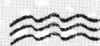

"The labyrinth is a sacred device, and walking these magical single-path mazes is yet another way to get in touch with your intuition."

LABYRINTHS

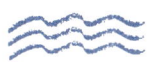

Labyrinths are another way to link the rational mind to the intuitive, spiritual aspect of our consciousness. Native Americans have used labyrinths for centuries. There are labyrinths that people walk the world over, or ones people build in their backyards. No doubt you've seen images of labyrinths all of your life. Would it surprise you to know that images of labyrinths have appeared in cave drawings the world over, and throughout time? The earliest labyrinth dates back to about 500 B.C. and is seen on Cretan coins. There must be something magical, or at least beyond our understanding, at work for these images to appear worlds apart. How could people of different ages, and different cultures, all spontaneously conceive of the same designs?

WHAT IS A LABYRINTH?

A labyrinth is a single-path maze. It can be as simple as three turns from the entrance to the center, or as complex as a winding, mile-long walk. Not all mazes are labyrinths. Remember the hedged maze in the movie *The Shining?* This is the kind of maze that confuses the person walking it—it has many paths and teases the walker by constantly diverging onto paths that lead back to the same point. It is the fact that there is only one path in a labyrinth maze that makes it special: there is only one way to go once you have embarked on the path. Many believe the labyrinth is a sacred device, and that walking these magical single-path mazes is yet another way to get in touch with the intuition.

Labyrinths can be circular in shape, or square, but often they adhere to a sacred geometry: using measurements that are "transcendental numbers" that never resolve, they just go on and on. The idea is that since these numbers can never be described in the physical world, they take us to a different plane. Also, dowsers have discovered that many of the ancient labyrinths were built on power centers (remember the ley lines?). Many people dowse to determine where to build their labyrinth. Some believe that the labyrinth itself creates energy fields once it has been built.

Labyrinths are used in two ways. People use labyrinths drawn on paper, and color them or "walk" them by tracing them with their finger to derive benefits. Others swear by the meditative joys of walking an actual three-dimensional labyrinth. I'll show you how to do both.

DRAWING A SEED PATTERN

Labyrinths are fairly simple to draw once you understand the basic concept. First, let's start with the seed pattern, or the classical three-circuit labyrinth, like the one found on the coins of ancient Crete. Take a blank sheet of paper and a pencil. Draw a vertical cross, with four dots at the outer edge of each quadrant (see figure). For a left-handed labyrinth all lines will be clockwise; for a right-handed labyrinth they will be counterclockwise. Put your pencil at the top point of the cross and draw a line up and over, connecting it to the upper right dot. Now put your pencil on the dot in the upper left, and connect that (also drawing a curved line up and over) to the right, horizontal axis of the cross. Next, put your pencil on the left horizontal axis of the original cross, and connect that up and over to the dot on the lower right side. Finally, connect the remaining dot on the lower left to the remaining bottom vertical axis of the cross. Practice this several times until you can do it without reading the directions, until the connections are intuitive. This is known as a left-

LABYRINTHS

Follow the steps above to draw your own 3-circuit labyrinth.

A finished 3-circuit labyrinth.

handed labyrinth because the first turn you would make if you were walking such a labyrinth, would be to your left.

You can now practice the reverse version—a right-handed labyrinth—by simply reversing the direction you draw the connections. Start at the top, but go to the left. Do this several times as well, until you're a natural.

This is called a three-circuit labyrinth because there are three paths you take to reach the center, or the "goal." A path is the circular route you walk in one direction, before having to make a turn and double back in the opposite direction. Can you number the three paths on your seed-pattern labyrinth? Check it against the numbers in the figure.

DRAWING THE CLASSICAL SEVEN-CIRCUIT LABYRINTH

Now that you're a pro at the seed pattern, let's try a slightly more complex labyrinth: the classical seven-circuit labyrinth. You'll notice that the starting pattern looks familiar—it's just the seed pattern with an extra set of L's dividing each quadrant (see figure.) Start the way you did with the seed pattern: put your pencil at the tip of the cross, and curve it clockwise up and over, but this time, connect it to the top of the L. Now connect the top of the L in the upper left quadrant to the dot in the upper right quadrant, and so on. Do you see the pattern? Notice that each time, you simply go back to the next open line or dot, working your way counterclockwise down the left side, and connect it to the next open line or dot working your way clockwise along the right side. It's quite simple once you get the hang of it. Do you notice something satisfying, or especially calming about the predictability of it? Even *drawing* a labyrinth can be soothing.

Again, make several left-handed labyrinths, and then reverse it and make several right-handed labyrinths.

LABYRINTHS

Some labyrinths are squared off, or have sharp angles at the turns, some weave back and forth more on one side than the other. But these two classical forms are ideal for exercises to get in touch with your intuition.

Follow the steps above to draw your own 7-circuit labyrinth.

Powers That Be

1 = Yellow	5 = Violet
2 = Orange	6 = Indigo
3 = Red	7 = Blue
4 = Green	8 = Magenta

The 7-circuit labyrinth completed. To color a 7-circuit labyrinth follow the colors indicated by the numbers shown in the chart above.

COLORING THE LABYRINTH

Coloring a blank labyrinth can be very therapeutic. Think of a question that's been troubling you. It can be as simple as, "Should I buy a new couch," or as personal as, "Should I break up with my boyfriend." Think about this question as you begin coloring the blank labyrinth. Let whatever thoughts or feelings come up as you continue to color in the labyrinth. Don't try to analyze it. Many people find this to be a powerful exercise. It can bring up physical feelings (a headache) or emotional feelings (frustration, anger, joy). It can help you clarify your thoughts, or it can unravel all the confusions and expectations you may have attached to the question you're pondering. Don't stop until you've finished coloring the labyrinth. When you're done, take a deep breath and assess what you're feeling. Maybe write down your impressions from the exercise.

Don't make any decisions right away. Let the experience sit with you for a while. Often, the meaning of the feelings that come up takes a day or two to become clear. Maybe you felt teary or emotional while coloring because the couch is associated with lots of family memories you're not ready to let go of. Maybe you felt energetic and joyful because you are ready to let go of the old and allow new things in your life. Perhaps you've been ready to break up with your boyfriend because he's not everything you think he should be—successful in his career, or ready to get married—but drawing the labyrinth and thinking of leaving him made you feel anxious and unhappy because you realized that he's kind and loving and makes you happy right now. Sometimes doing labyrinth work helps you focus on the present, rather than project mentally into the future. We can often get caught up in our heads, overanalyzing our expectations of what our lives and the people in them should be doing. Concentrating on something as simple as coloring a maze can help us focus our attention and tap in to our feelings on the here and now.

HOW TO MAKE A LABYRINTH

Many believe that the best way to work with labyrinths is to walk them. But to do that, you need to build one—unless you happen to live near a sacred labyrinth site that's available to you! Don't worry, it's not as much of an undertaking as it sounds, and most people find the project of building their own labyrinth satisfying. Here are some easy ways to do it. If you have a blacktop or driveway, it's as simple as setting up a game of hopscotch. Take some colored chalk and practice drawing a giant version of the seed pattern and classical seven-circuit pattern you drew with pencil on paper. You can draw one in the sand, at the beach, or on a dirt patch with a stick.

If you're building a labyrinth on a lawn or on a cleared plot of dirt or sand, you can build it with pebbles and stones, or pieces of wood to use as the outline. Some people like to stake it out in the ground, driving sticks of about a foot tall vertically into the ground, thus creating mini walls for their labyrinth. Be creative. Make your labyrinth out of material that appeals to you, as long as you can see it clearly and the paths are easily delineated. After all, the whole point of using the labyrinth is that you don't have to think too hard about where you're going when you start walking it!

WALKING THE LABYRINTH

There are two ways to walk a labyrinth. You can "walk" a labyrinth that is drawn out on paper by tracing it with your index finger. Take your pointer finger and place it at the mouth, or entrance to the labyrinth (see figure). Now slowly trace the route to the center, not stopping until you get there. Once you reach the goal, pause for a moment. When you're ready, trace the route back, again without stopping.

The same basic technique works for actually walking a

labyrinth. Stand at the mouth, or entrance. Begin walking the path, slowly and purposefully. It should feel like a walking meditation. When you reach the center, or goal, breathe deeply. Stay there for as long as you like. Once you start back on the return path, don't stop until you've reached the mouth again.

Do you feel calmer? Many people find these exercises clear their minds because they are so focused on following the path, that all of their other cares and worries don't have time to creep into their thinking! Do you find that is true? Walking the labyrinth truly is a walking meditation. In fact, it helps many people who have trouble clearing their minds for meditation.

USING THE LABYRINTH TO SOLVE PROBLEMS

Enhancing meditation is one way labyrinths get us more in touch with our intuition. But the labyrinth can also be a powerful tool for accessing our intuition for actual problem solving. Think of something that has been on your mind. Labyrinths can often be helpful with problems that we tend to overanalyze, such as career questions. Consider the following questions, for instance:

- Is my current job the right job for me?
- Would I be happier changing careers?
- Should I ask for a raise and promotion?
- Should I quit my job and follow my dream to write my novel?
- Should I hire/fire [name of person]?
- Should I accept this new job I've been offered?

Let's look at the fourth question, one I'm sure many of us have mulled over in some incarnation—whether to write a novel, start a rock band, open a pie store, or become a dowser!

Recall that there are seven paths in the classical seven-circuit labyrinth. These paths correspond to the seven chakras. Sig

Lonegren, an expert in labyrinths, recommends linking the paths to the seven chakras, using key words for each path. One possibility, shown here, is numbering the labyrinth paths in the order in which you walk them. You enter on path 3, so your first path is 3, the second is 2, and you complete the labyrinth in this order: 3, 2, 1, 4, 7, 6, 5. The goal is 8, the center. The first path corresponds to the root chakra and the physical; the second path corresponds to the sacral chakra and the emotional; the third represents the solar plexus chakra and the mental; the fourth, the heart chakra and the personally spiritual; the fifth is the throat chakra and manifestation; the sixth, the brow chakra and vision; and the seventh, the crown chakra and God.

Note in the figure on page 96 that since we number each path from the outside in, you aren't really walking the paths in number order. The maze starts on the third path. Refer to this figure to help you identify what aspect of the problem you are to consider at each turn of the maze.

Stand at the mouth of the labyrinth (or place your finger at the entrance to your labyrinth on paper) and consider your problem or question. As you walk each path, you focus on only the aspect of the problem that corresponds to that path. Then, when you turn onto another path, ponder only the aspect of the problem that corresponds to the new path. It is a great way to get at your "gut instincts."

So let's begin, and use our sample question: Should I quit my job and pursue my dream to write a novel? The first path you take is number 3, the mental. The key phrase here is "I think." As you walk this path, answer the question, "What do I think about this?" Perhaps your rational mind tells you this is foolishness. You can't just quit your job. How will you pay your bills? You're an adult, you can't be so irresponsible.

Now you come to the first turn and you are on path 2, the emotional. The phrase here is "I feel." What do you feel about this question? Maybe you feel that you'd love to quit your job, it would be so wonderful not having to go to that office ever again! To just be able to devote yourself to your lifelong dream. Be aware of how this possibility makes you feel, physically: excited? joyful? anxious? Don't judge it. Just feel it.

Now you turn again and come to path 1, the physical. How would quitting your job and writing affect you on the physical level? Will you be able to pay for the roof over your head? The food for yourself and your family? Maybe your job is so physically stressful that leaving it would be beneficial to your health. What about health insurance? All of these are questions that relate to your physical world.

The next turn takes you to path 4, the spiritual. How would this decision affect your spiritual life? Maybe it would increase your sense of faith, because it would be a leap of faith to do this and believe you'll be taken care of, that everything will work out, that the universe is abundant. Maybe you will feel more connected to the creative life force if you are doing creative work. Whatever comes into your mind, trust these answers.

Path 7 is the next turn, the God path. On this short path, you ask for help from the God or spiritual force of your understanding. Simply ask for help and guidance.

The next turn is the critical turn, onto path 6, the vision path. As you walk this path, simply be open to whatever vision comes to you. This is where you may "see" the answer—or sense it. Maybe you'll see what your life could look like if you say "yes" to this question. Maybe it will look wonderful, maybe it will look terrible. Just be open to whatever you see. It may be a scene, a word, a sound, nothing. Whatever it is, trust it. Even if it's not what you want it to be. Even if the answer is "no."

For path 5, manifestation, you must trust the answer you got in path 6. Think of what you first have to do to carry that out. Maybe on path 6 you sensed you should quit your job. Now, on path 5, you get the message, "But not yet. Save some money, find some part-time work, then quit." Or perhaps you saw on path 6 that you shouldn't quit. So on path 5, you see ways to start improving your work situation. You could start waking up an hour earlier each day to write that novel. Or maybe the answer you saw was "Yes, get out of that job!" and on path 5 you start drafting your letter of resignation.

On the eighth turn you've reached the center of labyrinth, the goal. Breathe in deeply, relax. Take some time to let everything go before you turn back and wind your way back.

You're not done yet, though. There's more to do on the way back. The return trip is for thanking your intuitive or spiritual sources for guidance, and checking out how you feel about the answers you got. On the exit, you begin again on path 5, manifestation. Just think again about what you sensed or saw on this path on the way in. On path 6, vision, again, just think about the answer that came to you earlier. It's important not to judge yourself or your intuition at all! As you turn onto path 7, thank your God or spiritual force for the guidance it's provided. Turning onto path 4, ask yourself how this decision will affect your spiritual life, personally. Will it help you? Heading onto path 1, ask yourself if this solution will take care of all your physical needs. On path 2, check out how this decision feels—Are you happy? nervous? Do you feel good about the answer? Finally, on path 3, what do you think about this solution? Remember, these answers aren't foolproof. They're simply tools for getting at your intuition or subconscious. If your rational mind doesn't agree, don't do it! You need to feel right about the solution. Remember, all of the exercises in this book are to help you tap in to your intuition. You may need practice, or you may not be ready to do what your intuition tells you! The point is to have fun, not torture yourself with "shoulds!"

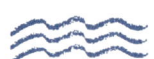

CHAPTER SEVEN

MIND AND BODY POWERS

*"The energy is within us
to become and achieve
all that we want, if we just learn
how to tap in to it."*

MIND AND BODY POWERS

THE ENERGY IN YOUR HANDS

By now you will hopefully be convinced that there is energy around us that we can't always see but can be powerful if we know how to tap in to it. What about energy within us? Auras show the energy that radiates around us, and we can dowse our chakras, the energy centers in our bodies. But, then, there is

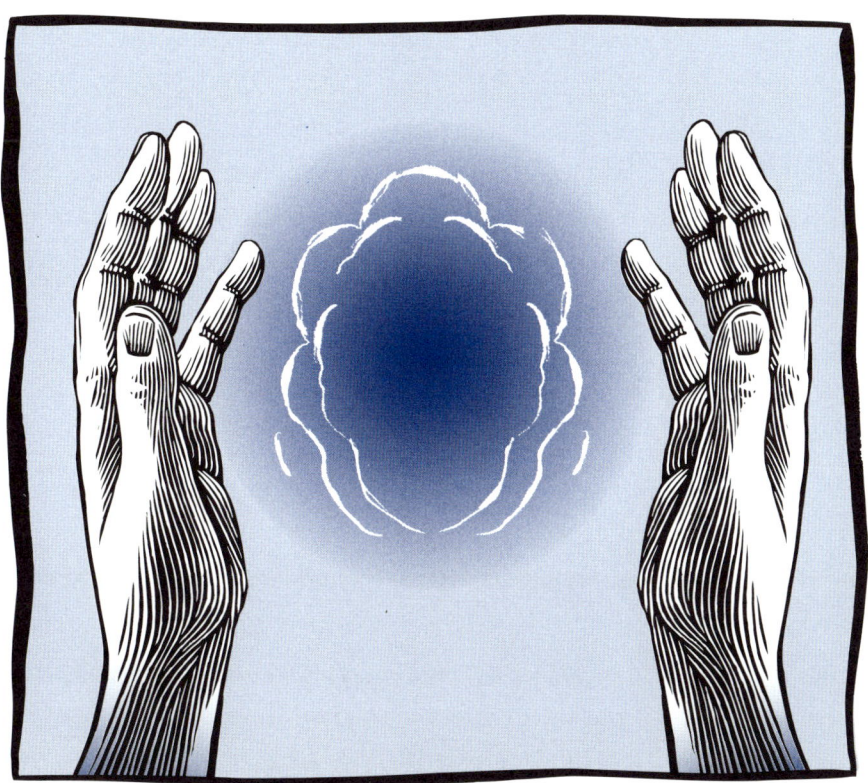

The hand chakras are so powerful you can feel the energy by just cupping the hands after vigorously rubbing the palms together for a few seconds.

also energy within our bodies and minds that can be powerful when focused. And you don't need to have special skills to harness it either—just a willingness to believe, and practice.

One of the most powerful energy zones for giving off and receiving energy is the hands. Hand and fingertip chakras are perhaps the most powerful of the secondary chakras. To activate the energy in your fingertip chakras, simply run the fingertips of one hand against the fingertips of the other hand quickly for ten to thirty seconds. Slowly push your fingertips toward each other. You should be able to feel energy coming off of them.

You can do the same thing to activate the hand chakras. Rub your palms together vigorously for ten to thirty seconds. Now cup your hands as if you are holding a ball in front of you, with your palms facing toward each other. Move your hands in and out, away from and toward each other. Do you feel anything? Does it feel like a warm ball of energy between your hands?

HEALING A HEADACHE WITH YOUR HANDS

You can put energy into a person, or pull energy out of a person with the energy in your hands or fingers. You may have heard of or experienced Reiki, a therapy used for healing and stress reduction that doesn't even involve actual touch, but just holding the hands very close to certain areas of a person's body. A simple way to feel the power of touch is to try healing a headache with your hand energy.

The next time someone you know—who would be a willing and open participant—has a headache, try this. Rub your hands together vigorously to activate the hand chakras and your energy. Ask the person to sit up tall and relaxed. Have her breathe in deeply with her eyes closed. Now, while her eyes are closed tell her you are going to place your hands near her temples, but you won't touch her head. She may be able to feel your hands, even though you aren't touching her. Keep your hands placed near her temples and concentrate on pulling the clogged,

Mind and Body Powers

You can use the energy in your hands to heal a headache—pull the bad energy out and send the good energy in.

painful energy that is causing her headache away. You may feel the pain come into your hands. If you do, don't let it move above your wrists. You can project it out into the universe by pointing your hands away and imagining the energy leaving them. You may also send new energy in from your hands. Usually, after just five minutes, the headache has melted away.

LEVITATING WITH YOUR FINGERTIPS

Do you remember slumber parties or Halloween parties where you played spooky games and tried to levitate your friends? Do you remember how surprised you were when it worked? Maybe you don't recall whether it worked; maybe you figured someone was lifting more than his share. Well, it is possible to lift people with just your fingertips when you focus all of your concentration and energy. This is an example of how pow-

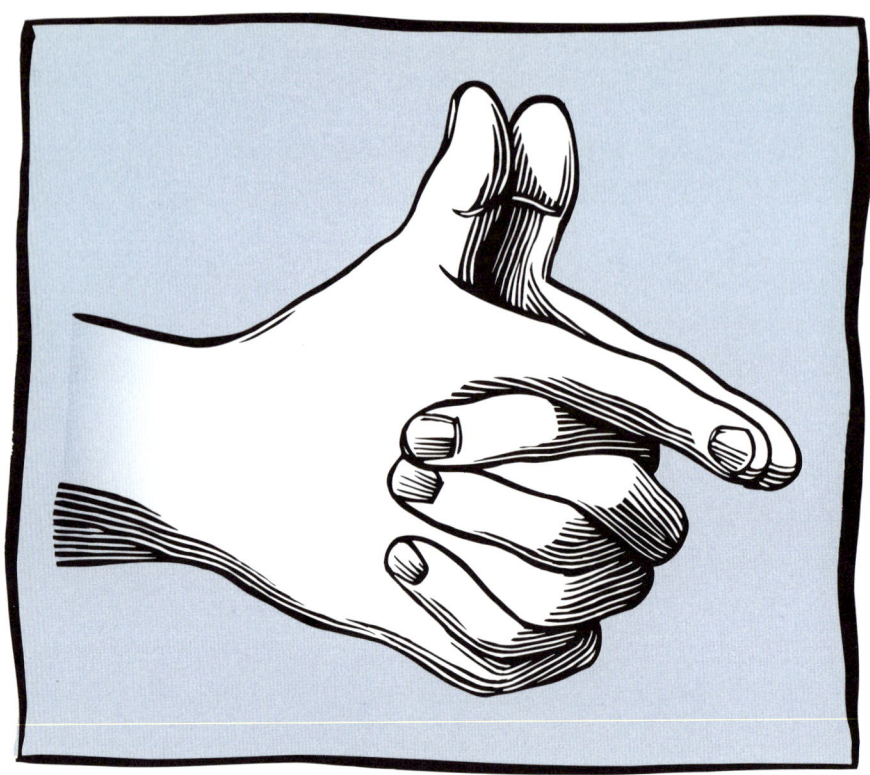

You can use your fingertips to levitate a friend by clasping your hands together and extending your two index fingers as shown.

erful the mind can be when you focus attention. If you can lift a large person off a table or chair with the powers of your mind, imagine what you can do if you direct your attention to specific goals in your life!

There are two ways I like to demonstrate this powerful phenomenon. The first requires six people. Have one person lie down flat on a table. The other five of you stand around the person: two on each side near the "patient's" knees, two on each side of the waist, and one at the top of the head. Have each levitator clasp his hands together and extend his index fingers. (Or, the five levitators could just extend the index and middle fingers of each hand facing up.) Place the fingers beneath the spot you are standing (under each knee, each side of the waist, and under the top of the head). Now, all five of you, including the subject laying on the table, take three deep breaths together: in and out, in and out, in and out. After the third exhale, inhale and hold the breath at the same time with the intent of lifting the person in the air. Lift as you hold the breath: the person will raise

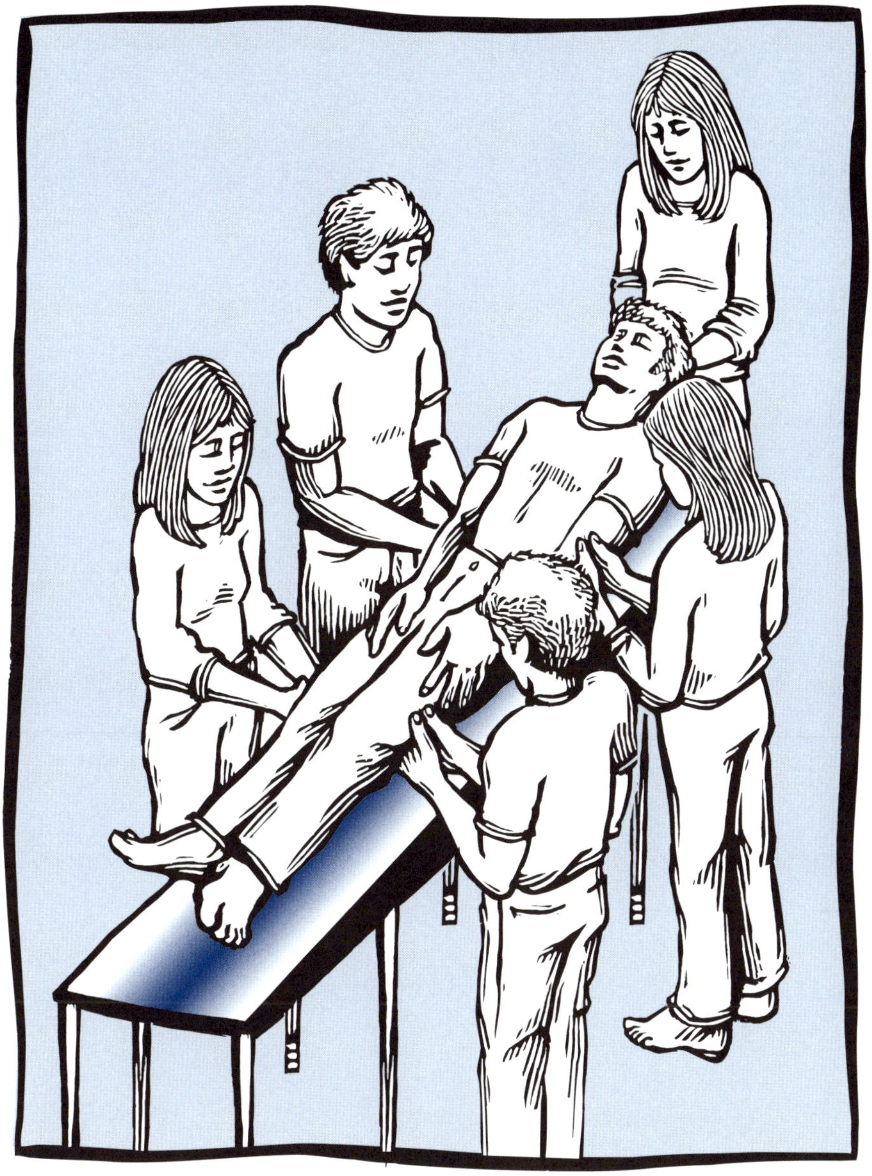

MIND AND BODY POWERS

Position five people at key points around the "subject" lying on a table: at each knee, each side of the waist, and at the head. This is not just a party trick–using only your fingers and lifting all together in unison, watch the "subject" rise easily.

right up off the table! If it doesn't work the first time, practice the three deep breaths, holding the last breath with focused attention, a few times and then try again.

With the second method, you need five people. The subject sits in a chair. Two people stand on each side of the person in the chair: two in line with each shoulder and two in line with each knee. The lifters place their clasped hands with index fingers extended (see illustration on page 110) under each armpit, and

Just four people can lift someone—even someone much heavier than they are—right out of a chair and overhead if all concentrate and work together. I've seen four slight women lift a two-hundred-pound man this way.

under each knee. Have them try to lift the person: no doubt, they can't budge the subject. Now, each person places his left hand, palm facing down, above the subject's head, one on top of the other, one at a time (careful not to touch each other's hands). Then do the same with the right hands. So the order is: left hand, over left hand, over left hand, over left hand, then right hand, over right hand, over right hand, over right hand. Now everyone takes a deep breath in and then pulls their hands away, very quickly, in the exact reverse order in which they extended their hands and *immediately* places their pointed index fingers under the person and lifts—you'll float that person right up off the chair.

I was at a party once when a telephone repair man, weighing over two hundred pounds, thought this was the funniest thing he'd ever heard. There was no way it would work with him, he said. He was so convinced, he agreed to try it. Four small young women volunteered to be the lifters. First, they couldn't budge him, of course. Then they did the exercise and floated him way up off the chair. His eyes got big as he sat a foot off his seat. He never said another word!

MIND OVER MATTER

Ever wonder how people are able to walk on hot coals, karate chop a piece of wood with their bare hands, even bend metal by just concentrating very hard? Are these tricks? No. These are things people actually can do when they, literally, put their minds to it. With proper training, people can train their minds to shut out pain, and even send focused energy to other objects to affect their physical makeup!

For many people, when you say spoon bending, Uri Geller is the name that comes to mind. He was quite famous in the 1970s, appearing on television numerous times to demonstrate his psychic abilities. Skeptics thought he was nothing more than a clever magician, and even a few psychics thought he gave their calling a bad name. I don't pretend to know the answer. But I have witnessed some "normal" people who can achieve the same mindbending results with spoon bending! In fact the publisher of this book has twisted at least a half dozen spoons at will.

Try the following. Take a spoon from your kitchen drawer (better not take a piece of good silver). Focus your energy on a certain spot on the spoon that you want to bend. Say "bend, bend, bend, bend" over and over to help focus your attention. Then when you feel that you've really concentrated your complete, undivided attention, and sent energy to that spot on the spoon, try to bend it with your hands. I've found that not every-

The Truth Within Your Arms

You can see how your body's energy can be used as a lie detector by following this simple exercise. Just like you programmed your pendulum or L-rods you can program yourself to give "true" and "false" answers to questions. To do this, you'll need a partner. Hold one arm straight out to your side. (If you prefer, you can use both arms, and stand like a giant T.) Tell yourself you want your arm to be strong for "true" and weak for "false" when your partner tries to press down on your arm. Indicate the correct responses at least once: hold your arm out firmly and have your partner press down strongly, but not too hard. Resist your partner's pressure, keeping your arm in place. This is the "true" response. Now have your partner press on your arm again, and this time, let it respond to the pressure, drooping downward. This is the "false" response. Now have your partner test you with some questions. Start with ones you can test your response to. Here are some examples:

Is ____ your first name?
Are you a female?
Are you ____ years old?
Are you married?
Do you have children?
Do you have a sister? more than one? more than two?
Do you have a brother? more than one? more than two?

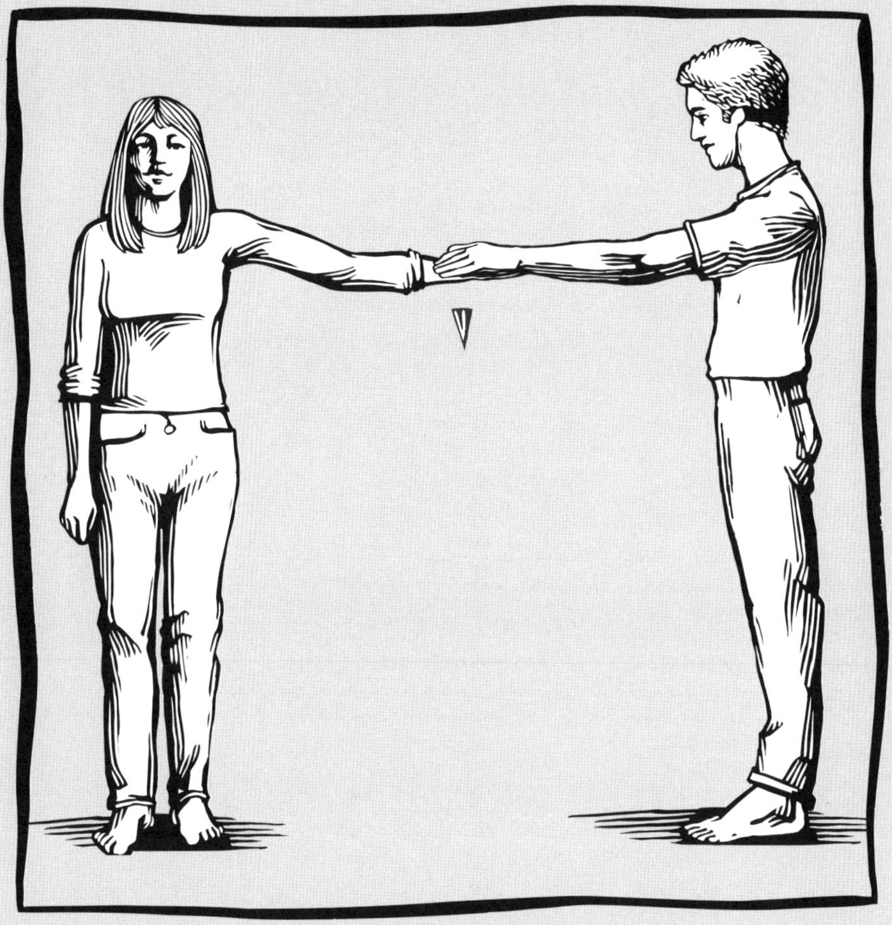

Mind and Body Powers

Once you feel your arm is responding properly, you can have fun with some more subjective questions, such as:

> *Do you like to travel?*
> *Will you take a vacation? to a foreign country?*
> *Do you speak a foreign language? more than one?*
> *Do you like to read? fiction? non-fiction?*
> *Will you get married?*
> *Will you have children? in one year? two years? etc.?*
> *Have you lived in this town over _____ years?*
> *Will you own a house one day? in one year? five years? etc.?*
> *Will you ever be rich?*
> *Will you ever be famous?*

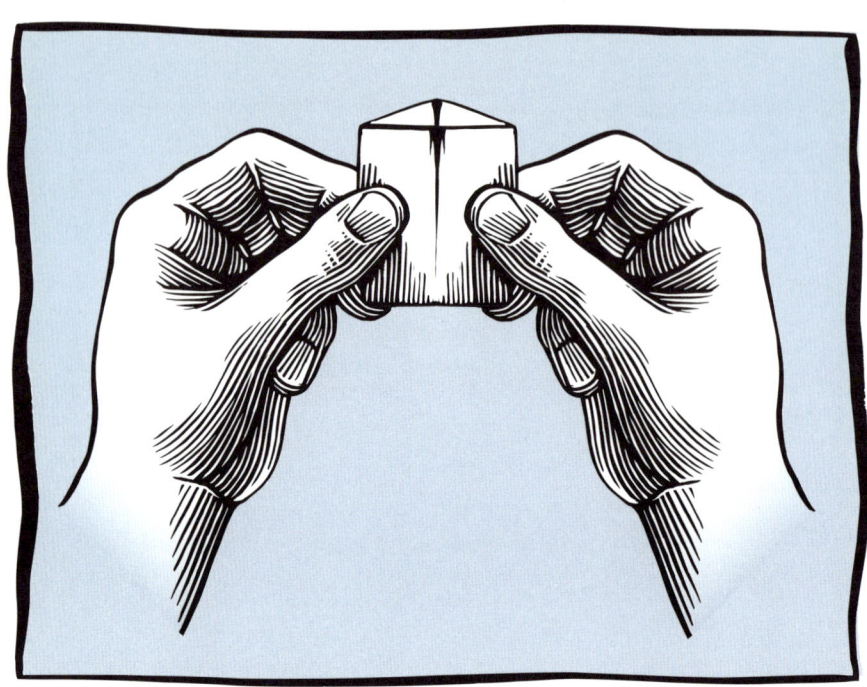

Use the two colored pencil holders included in the kit to illustrate the energy around us that we can put to good use. Press the two pencil holders firmly together for 45–50 seconds. You will meet some resistance when you try to pull them apart.

one can do this. To be honest, I myself have never had much luck with it. But my wife, who was highly skeptical of the exercise, was trying it for the heck of it one day and was astounded to see the metal go limp like a piece of wet spaghetti within seconds.

What makes this happen? I have no idea. But once again, there's energy flying in and around us that, when harnessed, can be powerful. Another fun example is the way some people can seemingly magnetize, or electrify their face in a way that coins, or other metals (again, you can try a spoon, but coins are less cumbersome) literally stick to it. Take some coins, or a spoon, and lay them out in front of you. Now, focus your mind's eye on your face. Feel the energy flowing through your cheeks. You should start to feel a tingle. Slowly take the coins and stick them to your cheeks or forehead. You may have to tilt your head back slightly at first. But once they're in place, while still keeping your attention focused on the energy in your face keeping those coins in place, you should be able to slowly move your face—the coins will remain stuck. If you lose your concentration, what happens? In all likelihood, the coins fall off.

One of the best ways to illustrate the energy that we can use to "charge" things around us, is the exercise using the colored pencil holders in your kit. Take the colored pencil holders, one in each hand. Hold each one between your thumb and index finger. Now, line them up with each other, the longest sides touching. Pull them apart. There's no resistance, right? You can see that we're not tricking you with magnetized pencil holders. Now, again press the two pencil holders together, with equal force, as hard as you can, pushing hard and continuously. Count to forty-five slowly. Then try to pull them apart. Can you feel the force keeping them together? If you've done it correctly, you should feel resistance, like you can't pull them apart at first. If it didn't work, try it again, and press the two pencil holders together for longer this time.

DEVELOPING ESP

We all have the ability to be at least slightly psychic. Have you ever had a "bad feeling" that something was wrong, only to find out later that a friend or family member was sick, or had something happen to them? Have you ever thought about someone you hadn't seen in a long time, and then gotten a phone call, or a letter—or seen them unexpectedly that very day? We tend to brush off these events as coincidences. Couldn't it be that there's energy out there that our minds take in without us knowing it? Many believe that this is all that "ESP" is. It's not an extra sense, it's more like being extra sensitive: tuning in the mind and the other senses, opening up the intuition, so that we're extra sensitive to energy and the messages it carries from the world around us.

Many people who work to develop ESP or psychic skills believe that it's simply extending the main senses in a way that allows the images, sounds, smells, tastes, and tactile information to carry the extra information to our consciousness. Is that really so hard to believe? Think of how people who have a deficiency in one sense (being blind or deaf) develop heightened

Edgar Cayce

Edgar Cayce, who lived from 1877 to 1945, became world famous for his psychic readings. As a young school boy in Kentucky, he was able to learn his school lessons by sleeping on his books. (If only we could all learn this skill!) His first true healing experience was when at age twenty-one he developed a throat problem and was told he would lose his voice forever. He put himself in the sleep-like trance he'd learned in his childhood and was able to tell doctors what they should do to heal him. And it worked.

He realized he could do similar "readings" for others, by putting himself into a sleep-like trance in order to answer people's questions. The accuracy of his intuitive powers soon amazed people. His early readings focused mainly on medical problems, but over time he covered topics ranging from dreams, meditation, and prophecy to other subjects. He recommended meditation for its spiritual and mental benefits decades before it caught on in the United States. Edgar Cayce's readings—he did over 14,000—were transcribed and have been the basis for hundreds of books, and continue to be researched and studied.

---

sensitivity of the other senses. Why can't we all do this if we work on it? For instance, many people can feel colors, or get a taste from things they put in their hands.

See if you can use your heightened sense of touch to help you perceive color. Cut some squares, about three inches by three inches (exact size isn't important, this is just a manageable size) from different pieces of colored paper. Stick with strong hues: red, orange, blue, green, black, yellow. Now, rub your hands together for about thirty seconds to stimulate your hand chakras and your sensitivity. Pick just two colors to begin with. Put one hand over each different colored square. With each square, wait until you get a sense of the color. How does purple feel? Often it feels cool, whereas yellow, for instance, may feel warmer. But there are no rules. Note carefully how each color feels for you.

Take your time getting to know your feeling for each color. Once you feel you have a sense of the two colors, close your eyes, or blindfold yourself, and have someone put each color before you. See if you can correctly feel the color by holding your palm over the card. Remember, you have a 50 percent chance of getting the answer right, so you need several trials before knowing if you're really feeling the colors. We have included four squares of colored paper in your kit: purple, yellow, pink, and green.

Other people believe ESP is the result of focused concentration and sending thoughts or images to another person. This is the "mind reading" type of ESP. For instance, Mary Sinclair, wife of the American novelist Upton Sinclair, believed she had ESP skills. She had her husband test her skills by having him draw a picture, and then think about the image and try to send it to her telepathically. Her method was to combine concentration with relaxation in order to receive telepathic images. She would focus on one mental picture, which would clear her mind and put her into a deep, relaxed state. This is similar to what people do when they practice transcendental meditation. In this state, she would receive whatever images or thoughts came to her. Sinclair published a book called *Mental Radio* (which was, in fact, what they were trying to achieve) that showed the results of their tests. She was often wrong in terms of interpreting what he was sending her, but if you look at the figures, she was remarkably accurate in capturing the images themselves! This shows how we have to be open to our intuition, but not make too many judgments or jump to too many conclusions about what we see.

CONCLUSION

I hope you've had some fun with these "games," and that I've got you thinking about the amazing powers that we can't see, but are out there, buzzing around and inside us. As a longtime dowser and the president of the American Society of Dowsers for two terms, I've seen these powers touch people in many ways. Type A personalities have been able to relax and "go with the flow" as they tune in to the powers that are around and within them—and beyond their understanding. People's worlds go from being quite narrow, to creative and expansive beyond anything they could have imagined.

I've been impressed time and again with what people can achieve when they start to harness the power of learning to focus their attention and their minds on their goals and dreams. The energy is within us to become and achieve all that we want, if we just learn to tap in to it. That's what dowsing has taught me. I hope this kit starts you out on a path that helps you believe that though we may not understand all the powers in this world, they can still be used to our advantage.